Robert Carrier's Quick Cook

CONTENTS

INTRODUCTION

Take A Little Ingenuity;
And A Spirit Of Adventure;
Blend In A Little Willingness
To Experiment . . . And
You'll Find You've
Created Something Wonderful.

It has been said that to serve a truly memorable meal you need both skill and flair. I don't agree that this is as impossible as it sounds. Skill can be acquired and you can develop flair even if you weren't born with it. You simply need basic knowledge to blend and serve foods that complement each other in flavour, taste, colour and texture. And there is no denying that there is great joy in transforming everyday raw ingredients into an exciting meal—one that first pleases the eye and then the palate.

We all admit that an everyday dinner at home can become a humdrum and repetitious affair, but there is no law that says it has to stay that way. Never has there been such a supply of superb frozen, canned and fresh foods, such a wealth of domestic and imported herbs, spices and delicacies, such a variety of gleaming new electric kitchen equipment for you to use and enjoy. By adding a little more imagination and a little love to your cooking, you, your family and friends can dine as well in your own home as those who eat in the world's best restaurants (my own included).

This book is devoted to recipes that can be prepared in thirty minutes by the reasonably accomplished amateur cook. Of course, if this is your first attempt at Carrier cooking, it might take a little longer. For if you have never chopped an onion, peeled a carrot, or cut a cucumber into thin *julienne* strips, you will have to 'get your hand in' as my grandmother used to say. Then once you get the feel of the recipes and learn to wield your kitchen knife with a little more dexterity, you will find that this book is a treasure trove of delectable and attractive new ideas guaranteed to bring your cooking—quickly and easily—up to star status.

The only exception to the quick cooking rule is my recipe for *glace de viande*—a professional cook's aid that is, I'm afraid, expensive to make and takes a long time simmering on top of the stove or in the lowest of ovens; but is well worth all the expense and effort involved when you see what it will do for your simplest recipes. With just a teaspoon or two of this magic ingredient swirled into the pan at the last minute with a spoonful of diced butter and a squeeze of lemon juice, your quickly cooked steaks, chops, liver or fish will acquire a new dimension. Even a simple hamburger becomes interesting with a hint of *glace* in the pan juices. Try it, too, to add excitement to soups, sauces, casseroles and pasta dishes. You'll find it well worth the trouble involved.

One of my favourite editors once gave me great pleasure when she told friends that her cooking had improved immeasurably since I started contributing a monthly food column to her magazine. All she'd done, she insisted, to create this new excellence was to make sure that she always had in her refrigerator a few new staples: two or three lemons; a small carton of double cream; a plastic bag containing a few spring onions or chives and a few sprigs of parsley and coriander; and a small container of *glace de viande* (page 10). Except for the last item, which does require a little extra time and effort every once in a while, the other ingredients are really rather run of the mill. I'd add freshly ground salt and pepper, the remains of a bottle of red or white wine carefully kept over from last night's dinner, and perhaps a sniff or two of Madeira or cognac from a nearby drinks cupboard. That's how easily greatness (in cooking, that is) can be achieved.

Useful Facts and Figures

NOTES ON METRICATION

When making any of the recipes in this book, follow only one set of measures as they are not interchangeable.

In this book quantities are given in metric and Imperial measures. Exact conversion from Imperial to metric measures does not usually give very convenient working quantities and so the metric measures have been rounded off into units of 25 grams. The table below shows the recommended equivalents.

Ounces	Approx g to nearest whole figure	Recommended conversion to nearest unit of 25
1	28	25
2	57	50
3	85	75
4	113	100
5	142	150
6	170	175
7	198	200
8	227	225
9	255	250
10	283	275
11	312	300
12	340	350
13	368	375
14	396	400
15	425	425
16 (1 lb)	454	450
17	482	475
18	510	500
19	539	550
20 (1$\frac{1}{4}$ lb)	567	575

Note When converting quantities over 20 oz, first add the appropriate figures in the centre column, then adjust to the nearest unit of 25. As a general guide, 1 kg (1000 g) equals 2.2 lb or about 2 lb 3 oz. This method of conversion gives good results in nearly all cases.

Liquid measures The millilitre has been used in this book and the following table gives a few examples.

Imperial	Approx ml to nearest whole figure	Recommended ml
$\frac{1}{4}$ pint	142	150 ml
$\frac{1}{2}$ pint	283	300 ml
$\frac{3}{4}$ pint	425	450 ml
1 pint	567	600 ml
1$\frac{1}{2}$ pints	851	900 ml
1$\frac{3}{4}$ pints	992	1000 ml (1 litre)

Spoon measures All spoon measures given in this book are level unless otherwise stated.

Oven Temperatures

The table below gives recommended equivalents.

	°C	°F	Gas Mark
VERY COOL	110	225	$\frac{1}{4}$
	120	250	$\frac{1}{2}$
COOL	140	275	1
	150	300	2
MODERATE	160	325	3
	180	350	4
MODERATELY HOT	190	375	5
	200	400	6
HOT	220	425	7
	230	450	8
VERY HOT	240	475	9

NOTES FOR AMERICAN AND AUSTRALIAN USERS

In America the 8-fl oz measuring cup is used. In Australia metric measures are now used in conjunction with the standard 250-ml measuring cup. The Imperial pint, used in Britain and Australia, is 20 fl oz, while the American pint is 16 fl oz. It is important to remember that the Australian tablespoon differs from both the British and American tablespoons; the table below gives a comparison. The British standard tablespoon, which has been used throughout this book, holds 17.7 ml, the American 14.2 ml, and the Australian 20 ml. A teaspoon holds approximately 5 ml in all three countries.

BRITISH	AMERICAN	AUSTRALIAN
1 teaspoon	1 teaspoon	1 teaspoon
1 tablespoon	1 tablespoon	1 tablespoon
2 tablespoons	3 tablespoons	2 tablespoons
3½ tablespoons	4 tablespoons	3 tablespoons
4 tablespoons	5 tablespoons	3½ tablespoons

AN IMPERIAL/AMERICAN GUIDE TO SOLID AND LIQUID MEASURES

Solid measures

IMPERIAL	AMERICAN
1 lb butter or margarine	2 cups
1 lb flour	4 cups
1 lb granulated or caster sugar	2 cups
1 lb icing sugar	3 cups
8 oz rice	1 cup

Liquid measures

IMPERIAL	AMERICAN
¼ pint liquid	⅔ cup liquid
½ pint	1¼ cups
¾ pint	2 cups
1 pint	2½ cups
1½ pints	3¾ cups
2 pints	5 cups (2½ pints)

THE FLAVOUR PIANO

It is no secret that French chefs use more liquid in their sauces—almost twice as much—and consequently cook them longer, than do most other cooks: and as a result of this concentration and blending of flavours, their sauces are more suave, more transparent and consequently more delicious.

Remember, no sauce is ready as soon as it thickens: sauces should be cooked much longer, to allow the flavours to improve by careful reduction. For our 'quick cook' method of making perfect sauces without over-long cooking, we are going to use one of the classical methods of the nineteenth century French kitchen—a magical cook's aid called *glace de viande* (see below). I always keep a little of this thick, rich, rubbery-textured reduction of meat stocks and juices in the refrigerator. You'll find it keeps almost indefinitely. It is almost magical what a teaspoon or two can do to improve your sauces, casseroles, soups, and even super-quick grilled and sautéed dishes. I like to use it as a flavour and texture additive for creamed meats, fish and vegetables . . . and even for pasta sauces.

Now, *glace de viande* cannot be made in a minute. A good *glace* requires reduction by long, slow simmering to bring it to perfection. But—and here is the bonus—it only has to be made every six to eight weeks. And you will have enough from one cooking to give containers of *glace* to three friends, who can then prepare the *glace* in turn, giving you back your bounty. In this way, four cooks can assure perfection throughout the year with only an occasional effort.

Secret number one is to use a tablespoon or two of *glace de viande* to give suavity and flavour to sauces and casseroles, and just a teaspoon or two to enhance a grilled or sautéed dish of meat, poultry or seafood.

Secret number two is to use a careful reduction of two liquid 'flavourers'—wine and stock. For a cream-based sauce or dish, reduce six tablespoons of white wine and six tablespoons of chicken stock to just a tablespoon or two of each, and stir into your finished sauce or dish. Conversely, for a darker, richer sauce, do the same with red wine and beef stock. You'll find that this will do a great deal to enhance the flavour of your sauce.

In professional kitchens, we use a further quartet of chef's flavouring tricks when we desire to embellish our sauces. For the high notes—if your sauce is too bland, not exciting enough even after you have added your reductions of stock and wine—just add a squeeze of lemon juice or a dash of Tabasco; and for the mellowers—to soften the flavour of your sauces—reduce (again that all-important word) six tablespoons of cream to one to two tablespoons, and stir this in with just a hint of Madeira or cognac. Follow these simple suggestions and you will find that you have completely revolutionised your cooking.

To make *glace de viande* you will need:

3.5 kg/8 lb beef and veal bones
1 large Spanish onion, cut in half
1 or 2 chicken carcasses
**225 g/8 oz carrots, cut into 5-cm/2-in
  pieces**
**1 head celery with leaves, cut into
  5-cm/2-in pieces**
3 medium-sized onions, cut into quarters
100 g/4 oz beef dripping
**2 (397-g/14-oz) cans peeled Italian
  tomatoes**
**bouquet garni (2 sprigs of parsley, sprig
  of thyme, bay leaf)**
12 black peppercorns

Ask your butcher to give you beef and veal bones with some meat on them, and ask him to chop them into 10 to 15-cm/4 to 6-in pieces; you'll have to give him warning.

Sear Spanish onion halves over a high heat, cut side down, until cut surfaces are dark brown.

Combine beef and veal bones, chicken carcasses, carrot and celery pieces, onion quarters and beef dripping in a roasting pan, and brown in preheated extremely hot oven (250 C, 500 F, gas 10): this will take about an hour. When bones are well browned, transfer them with a slotted spoon to a very large, thick-bottomed, flameproof stockpot. Pour 7 litres/12 pints water into pot and bring to the boil. Skim. Add browned vegetables, transferring them with a slotted spoon, then add charred onion halves, tomatoes, bouquet garni and black peppercorns. Simmer over the lowest of heats or in a cool oven (110 C, 225 F, gas $\frac{1}{4}$), for 12–16 hours, until liquid has reduced to 3.5 litres/6 pints, skimming two or three times during cooking time.

Pass stock through a muslin-lined sieve into a clean pot. Skim. Bring to the boil and boil for 2 hours, or until reduced to 1 litre/$1\frac{3}{4}$ pints, skimming when necessary. (The *glace de viande* is cooked when the surface area is entirely covered with bubbles and the liquid has a syrupy consistency.) Pass again through a muslin-lined sieve and pour into jars. Allow to cool. Store in the refrigerator until ready to use.

Do not worry if a thin layer of fat collects on the surface as this helps to preserve the *glace*, but do remove it before using.

The Flavour Piano – a collection of 'flavourers' to embellish your sauces

CHAPTER ONE

DRINKS AND CANAPÉS

Pina Colada

50 g/2 oz canned crushed pineapple with
  juice, chilled
40 ml/1½ fl oz light rum
2 tablespoons coconut cream
10 ice cubes
pineapple shell, chilled
slice of kiwi fruit
sprigs of mint

Combine chilled crushed pineapple with juice,
light rum, coconut cream and 10 ice cubes in
the container of an electric blender, and blend.
Pour into chilled pineapple shell; do not strain.
Add more ice cubes, if desired. Decorate with
kiwi fruit slice and sprigs of mint, and serve.

Serves 1

Whisky Sour

65 ml/2½ fl oz whisky
ice cubes
1 teaspoon gomme syrup
dash of grenadine
juice of ½ lemon
soda water (optional)
slice of orange
1 maraschino cherry

Half-fill a cocktail shaker with ice cubes.
Combine gomme syrup, grenadine, lemon
juice and whisky in shaker, cover and shake.
Strain into a chilled glass. Add a little soda

water, if desired. Decorate with orange slice
and maraschino cherry, and serve.

Serves 1

White Lady

ice cubes
25 ml/1 fl oz gin
15 ml/½ fl oz Cointreau
15 ml/½ fl oz lemon juice

Half-fill a mixing glass with ice cubes. Combine
all ingredients in glass and stir. Strain into an
ice-filled glass and serve.

Serves 1

Sangria

2 oranges
2 lemons or limes
50 g/2 oz sugar
1 bottle dry red or rosé wine, chilled
600 ml/1 pint soda water, chilled

Cut 1 orange and 1 lemon or lime into thin
slices. Squeeze juice from remaining fruits into
a pitcher. Stir in sugar, chilled red or rosé wine,
soda water and fruit slices. Pour into chilled
glasses and serve.

Serves 8

Hintlesham Bloody Mary

ice cubes
50 ml/2 fl oz vodka
dash of Worcestershire sauce
pinch of celery salt
drop of Tabasco sauce
25 ml/1 fl oz dry sherry
dash of lemon juice
100 ml/4 fl oz tomato juice

Half-fill a mixing glass with ice cubes. Combine all ingredients in glass and stir. Add more Worcestershire sauce, if desired. Strain into an ice-filled glass and serve.

Serves 1

Amaretto Sour

50 ml/2 fl oz amaretto
ice cubes
2 tablespoons lemon or lime juice
2 tablespoons sparkling grapefruit juice
slice of lemon
1 maraschino cherry

Half-fill a cocktail shaker with ice cubes. Combine amaretto and lemon or lime juice in shaker, cover and shake. Strain into a chilled glass. Add sparkling grapefruit juice, and additional ice cubes if desired. Decorate with lemon slice and maraschino cherry, and serve.

Serves 1

Planter's Punch

50 ml/2 fl oz dark rum
40 ml/1½ fl oz unsweetened pineapple juice
40 ml/1½ fl oz orange juice
1 tablespoon lemon or lime juice
1 tablespoon gomme syrup
dash of grenadine
ice cubes
stick of fresh pineapple

Combine first six ingredients in a cocktail shaker, cover and shake. Strain into an ice-filled glass. Decorate with stick of fresh pineapple and serve.

Serves 1

Frozen Daiquiri

40 ml/1½ fl oz light rum
25 ml/1 fl oz lime juice
1 teaspoon icing sugar
1 teaspoon Grand Marnier
10 ice cubes
slice of lime

Combine light rum, lime juice, icing sugar and Grand Marnier in the container of an electric blender. Cover, and with blender running, add ice cubes one at a time, blending until drink is a slushy mixture. Pour into a chilled glass; do not strain. Decorate with lime slice and serve.

Serves 1

CANAPÉ BASES

The bases in this section can be teamed with any of the toppings, spread and dips on pages 14 and 17.

READY-TO-USE

A variety of packaged, ready-to-use bread slices—pumpernickel, rye bread, Melba toast, French toast— as well as biscuits, crackers and pastry shells, may be purchased to use as quick canapés. Even large potato crisps can be used to make simple, attractive bases. All canapé bases, other than untoasted bread, should be crisp. If necessary, crisp or freshen bases in a preheated moderate oven (180 C, 350 F, gas 4) for about 10 minutes.

SAUTÉED BREAD BASES

A   Cut bread into desired shapes with a pastry cutter or with the rim of a wine glass. Sauté on one side in a little butter. Drain on absorbent kitchen paper. Spread plain sides with canapé toppings and spreads of your choice.

B   Cut bread as above. Toast one side. Sauté untoasted side in butter. Drain on absorbent kitchen paper. Spread sautéed side as desired.

Note Most people find that sautéed canapé bases are preferable to ordinary toasted ones— they do not absorb juices from toppings and spreads and have far more flavour. It is best to spread canapé bases within 30 minutes of serving time: allowing them to stand too long makes them limp and soggy.

PARTY PIECES

French Bread-Based Canapés

Take a loaf of French bread and slice it into rounds 5 mm/¼ in thick. Spread each round with softened butter and there's the starting point for one of your best—and easiest—parties. Top with canapé toppings and spreads of your choice.

White Bread-Based Canapés

For more delicate mixtures, cut out small rounds from sliced white bread with a pastry cutter or with the rim of a wine glass. Spread each round with softened butter and top as desired.

Savoury Bread Croustades

Cut an unsliced loaf of white bread into slices 2 cm/¾ in thick, then cut out rounds with a 5 to 6-mm/2 to 2½-in pastry cutter, or with the rim of a wine glass of the same size. Using a smaller cutter or glass, cut down the centre of each round to within 5 mm/¼ in of the bottom. Scoop out centres. Sauté bases in a mixture of butter and olive oil, or brush with melted butter, and bake in a preheated hot oven (230 C, 450 F, gas 8) until crisp and golden brown. If sautéeing, drain on absorbent kitchen paper. Fill bases with canapé toppings and spreads of your choice.

You'll need 6 to 8 canapés for each guest.

CANAPÉ TOPPINGS

The toppings in this section can be teamed with any of the bases on pages 14 and 17.

ANCHOVY CREAM   Combine 225 g/8 oz Philadelphia cream cheese and anchovy paste to taste. Spread thickly on canapé bases. Pat a little chopped parsley around edges of spread.

Canapé Toppings. From the top, left to right: Anchovy Cream, Cream Cheese and Smoked Salmon, Cream Cheese and Caviar, Cream Cheese and Black Olives, Smoked Eel, Crab Salad, Steak Tartare, Prawn Butter, Liver Spread, Mexican Avocado, Poor Man's 'Caviar', Ham and Chutney

CREAM CHEESE AND SMOKED SALMON
Combine 225 g/8 oz Philadelphia cream cheese
and enough soured cream to make a smooth
spread. Spread thickly on canapé bases. Cut
smoked salmon into thin strips and roll up.
Garnish bases with a roll of smoked salmon
and pat a little chopped smoked salmon around
edges of spread.

CREAM CHEESE AND CAVIAR   Combine 225 g/
8 oz Philadelphia cream cheese and enough
soured cream to make a smooth spread. Spread
thickly on canapé bases, leaving edges of bases
visible. Spread a little black or red caviar on
top, and garnish with finely chopped chives.

CREAM CHEESE AND BLACK OLIVES   Combine
225 g/8 oz Philadelphia cream cheese and
enough soured cream to make a smooth
spread. Spread on canapé bases. Garnish each
canapé with chopped black olives and a whole
olive.

SMOKED EEL   Remove skin and bones from
225 g/8 oz smoked eel. Combine smoked eel, 4
to 6 tablespoons double cream and 2 tablespoons olive oil in a mortar, and pound to a
smooth paste. Season to taste with lemon juice,
salt and cayenne. Spread on canapé bases and
garnish with chopped parsley.

CRAB SALAD   Combine 225 g/8 oz cooked
crabmeat (reserving choice bits for garnish)
and 4 to 6 tablespoons well-flavoured mayonnaise. Add 1 teaspoon finely chopped onion
and 1 tablespoon finely chopped parsley, and
season to taste with salt and freshly ground
black pepper. Spread on canapé bases. Garnish
with reserved choice bits of crabmeat and
sprinkle a little chopped parsley round the
edges.

STEAK TARTARE   Combine 225 g/8 oz freshly
minced raw sirloin and 2 tablespoons finely
chopped onion, and season to taste with

Worcestershire sauce, salt and freshly ground
black pepper. Spread on canapé bases. Garnish
with capers and diced onion.

PRAWN BUTTER   Combine 50 g/2 oz peeled
cooked prawns and 100 g/4 oz softened butter
in a mortar and pound to a smooth paste.
Season to taste with salt and cayenne. Spread
on canapé bases. Garnish with peeled cooked
prawns which you have dipped in lemon juice.

LIVER SPREAD   Cream 100 g/4 oz liver sausage and 50 g/2 oz softened butter. Flavour with
cognac and season to taste with freshly ground
black pepper. Spread on canapé bases. Garnish
with finely chopped olives or gherkins and a
whole olive or slice of gherkin.

MEXICAN AVOCADO   Combine 1 stoned and
peeled ripe avocado and a little onion, garlic
and lemon juice in the container of an electric
blender. Season to taste with cayenne. Blend to
a smooth paste. Spread on canapé bases.
Sprinkle chopped parsley round the edges.

POOR MAN'S 'CAVIAR'   Stone and finely chop
12 to 16 black olives. Spread canapé bases of
your choice with Anchovy Cream (page 14).
Top with finely chopped black olive 'caviar'.
Garnish with finely chopped parsley and a slice
of gherkin.

HAM AND CHUTNEY   Dice 3 slices cooked
ham. Finely chop 1 (191-g/6¾-oz) jar mango
chutney. Spread canapé bases of your choice
with a cream cheese and soured cream mixture.
Top with ham and chutney mixture.

FILLED CANAPÉ BASES

The bases in this section can be teamed with any of the toppings, spreads and dips on pages 14 and 17.

PASTA SHELLS

Cook large pasta shells as directed on packet until tender but still *al dente*. Drain and cool, then fill shells as desired.

BUTTON MUSHROOMS

Wipe button mushrooms clean with a damp cloth. Scoop out centres with a melon baller. Brush hollowed-out mushrooms with lemon juice and fill as desired.

PASTRY BASES

Use pastry of your choice. Roll pastry out 3 mm/$\frac{1}{8}$ in thick and cut it into rounds, rectangles, triangles, fingers, squares, or other fancy shapes. Bake in a preheated hot oven (230 C, 450 F, gas 8) until golden brown. Spread with canapé toppings and spreads of your choice.

For variety, sprinkle pastry before baking with allspice, cardamom, caraway seeds, coriander, cayenne, curry powder, mace, mustard powder, paprika, or freshly grated cheese.

HARD-BOILED EGGS

A   Cool hard-boiled eggs by plunging them into cold water as soon as they are cooked. Carefully remove shells, cut eggs in half lengthways and scoop out yolks. Fill with canapé toppings and spreads of your choice.

B   Cool and shell hard-boiled eggs as above and cut in half crossways. Cut a thin slice from the base of each half to make it stand securely. Scoop out yolks and fill as desired.

C   Cool and shell hard-boiled eggs as above. Using a sharp pointed knife, make a series of cuts in a zigzag pattern round the centre of the egg. Pull apart the two halves. Make a base as above, scoop out yolks and fill as desired.

D   Cool and shell hard-boiled eggs as above and cut into slices 5 mm/$\frac{1}{4}$ in thick. Top with canapé toppings and spreads of your choice.

SPREADS AND DIPS

The spreads and dips in this section can also be used as toppings, and can be teamed with any of the bases on pages 14 and 17.

Chopped Chicken Livers

8 chicken livers
25 g/1 oz chicken fat or butter
1 medium-sized onion, finely chopped
2 large hard-boiled eggs, chopped
2 teaspoons finely chopped parsley
salt and freshly ground black pepper

1.   Melt chicken fat or butter in a thick-bottomed frying pan and sauté finely chopped onion until soft but not coloured. Add chicken livers and sauté until golden brown.

2.   Chop sautéed chicken livers and combine with the onion and chopped hard-boiled eggs. Add finely chopped parsley and season to taste with salt and freshly ground black pepper.

3.   Transfer chicken liver mixture to a serving dish and moisten, if necessary, with a little extra melted chicken fat or butter. Chill before serving.

Serves 4

Chopped Chicken Livers and Mushrooms

8 chicken livers
50 g/2 oz button mushrooms, sliced
25 g/1 oz chicken fat or butter
2 tablespoons cognac or Madeira
1 teaspoon onion juice
salt and freshly ground black pepper
2 tomatoes, peeled, deseeded and cut into
  5-mm/$\frac{1}{4}$-in dice
juice of $\frac{1}{2}$ lemon
1 teaspoon each finely chopped chives
  and parsley

1. Melt chicken fat or butter in a thick-bottomed frying pan and sauté chicken livers until golden brown. Remove from pan with a slotted spoon. Sauté sliced mushrooms in remaining fat until golden brown. Stir in cognac or Madeira. Remove mushrooms from pan with a slotted spoon. Reserve cooking liquids.

2. Finely chop chicken livers and mushrooms and combine with reserved cooking liquids. Add onion juice, and season to taste with salt and freshly ground black pepper.

3. Combine finely chopped chicken livers and mushrooms, diced tomatoes and lemon juice.

4. Transfer chicken liver and mushroom mixture to a serving dish. Moisten, if necessary, with a little extra melted chicken fat or butter, and sprinkle with finely chopped chives and parsley. Chill before serving.

Serves 4

Curry Dip

250 ml/8 fl oz mayonnaise
1 teaspoon finely chopped onion
1 teaspoon prepared horseradish
1 teaspoon tarragon vinegar
1 teaspoon curry powder
pinch of cayenne
cauliflower and broccoli florets, or other
  crisp vegetables

1. Combine mayonnaise, finely chopped onion, prepared horseradish, tarragon vinegar, curry powder and cayenne. Transfer to a serving bowl. Chill.

2. Serve dip surrounded by cauliflower and broccoli florets, or other crisp vegetables.

Serves 4

Guacamole

1 large ripe avocado pear
1 tablespoon lemon juice
1 teaspoon Worcestershire sauce
$\frac{1}{2}$ teaspoon salt
$\frac{1}{2}$ teaspoon finely chopped onion
$\frac{1}{4}$ teaspoon crushed garlic
generous pinch of cayenne
Melba toast and assorted biscuits

1. Cut avocado pear in half, remove stone and peel avocado. Sprinkle flesh with lemon juice, to preserve colour, and mash well with a fork.

2. Add Worcestershire sauce, salt, onion, garlic and cayenne to mashed avocado. Mix well. Transfer to a serving bowl and chill.

3. Serve guacamole surrounded by Melba toast and assorted biscuits.

Serves 2

Soured Cream and Caviar Dip

300 ml/½ pint soured cream
50 g/2 oz red caviar
150 g/5 oz cottage cheese
lemon juice
dash of Tabasco sauce
2 teaspoons finely chopped onion
potato crisps, crackers, biscuits,
  pumpernickel or Melba toast

1.   Soften cottage cheese with a fork. Add soured cream, lemon juice to taste, and Tabasco and finely chopped onion.

2.   Transfer dip to a serving bowl. Sprinkle with red caviar. Chill.

3.   Serve dip surrounded by potato crisps, crackers, biscuits, pumpernickel or Melba toast.

Serves 4 to 6

FINISHED CANAPÉS

Bacon and Tomato Canapés

8 rashers bacon, finely diced and sautéed
  until crisp
12 thin slices tomato
6 tablespoons mayonnaise
6 slices white bread
12 thin slices cucumber, cut into thin
  strips
12 thin slices stuffed olives

1.   Preheat grill to high.

2.   Combine finely diced and sautéed bacon and mayonnaise.

3.   Cut bread into 12 rounds the same size as the tomato slices. Toast bread rounds under preheated grill.

4.   Mound bacon and mayonnaise mixture on to toasted bread rounds.

5.   Remove seeds and pulp from tomato slices, leaving just the tomato 'ring'. Place a tomato 'ring' on top of each canapé, top with cucumber strips and garnish with a slice of stuffed olive. Chill before serving.

Makes 12

Provençal Canapé Rounds

40 g/1½ oz butter
3 tablespoons olive oil
1 medium-sized onion, finely chopped
1 clove garlic, mashed to a smooth paste
1 (425-g/15-oz) can peeled Italian
  tomatoes, drained and chopped, juice
  reserved
2 tablespoons tomato purée
½ teaspoon dried thyme
½ teaspoon dried oregano
salt and freshly ground black pepper
100 g/4 oz frozen puff pastry, defrosted
1 (50-g/1¾-oz) can anchovy fillets,
  drained and cut into thin strips
12 black olives, stoned and sliced

1.   Preheat oven to moderately hot (190 C, 375 F, gas 5).

2.   Melt butter with olive oil in a thick-bottomed saucepan and sauté finely chopped onion until soft but not coloured. Add mashed garlic, together with chopped tomatoes and reserved juice, tomato purée, dried thyme and oregano. Season to taste with salt and freshly ground black pepper. Cook for 15 to 20 minutes, or until smooth and thick.

3. Meanwhile, roll out puff pastry on a lightly floured board to a thickness of 3 mm/⅛ in. Using a floured (4-cm/1½-in) round pastry cutter, cut out 12 rounds. Lay them, 2.5 cm/1 in apart, on a dampened baking sheet.

4. Spread tomato sauce over pastry rounds and cook in preheated oven for 5 minutes, or until pastry is golden brown and sauce is bubbling. Garnish each round with a lattice of anchovy strips dotted with sliced black olives, and serve immediately.

Makes 12

Grilled Apple Croustades

2 small dessert apples
lemon juice
6 slices white bread
65 g/2½ oz butter
6 slices salami, rind removed
6 thin slices Cheddar cheese, trimmed to
  same size as salami slices
paprika

1. Preheat grill to high.

2. Peel and core apples. Slice each apple into three even-sized rings about 1 cm/½ in thick. Sprinkle with lemon juice to preserve colour.

3. Using a 6 to 7.5-cm/2½ to 3-in pastry cutter, or the rim of a wine glass, cut out a round from each bread slice.

4. Melt 25 g/1 oz butter in a thick-bottomed frying pan and sauté apple rings on both sides until golden brown. Drain on absorbent kitchen paper.

5. Melt remaining butter in another pan and sauté bread circles on both sides until crisp and golden brown. Drain on absorbent kitchen paper.

6. Place an apple ring on each sautéed bread slice. Cover each ring with a salami slice and top with a Cheddar cheese round. Sprinkle each croustade with a small pinch of paprika and grill under preheated grill until cheese is golden brown and bubbling. Serve immediately.

Makes 6

Raw Minced Beef Canapés

225 g/8 oz lean sirloin or rump steak,
  trimmed and minced
½ teaspoon onion juice
pinch of cayenne
1 teaspoon Worcestershire sauce
juice of ½ lemon
salt and freshly ground black pepper
6 slices rye bread, crusts removed
12 anchovy fillets, cut into 4 equal-sized
  strips
1 (25-g/1-oz) jar capers, drained

1. Preheat grill to high.

2. Combine minced sirloin or rump steak, onion juice, cayenne, Worcestershire sauce and lemon juice, and season to taste with salt and freshly ground black pepper.

3. Toast rye bread slices under preheated grill. Cut each slice into four squares.

4. Spread raw minced beef mixture on to toasted bases. Garnish with a cross of anchovy strips, place 1 caper in the centre of each square and serve.

Makes 24

CHAPTER TWO

APPETISERS AND SNACKS

PROVENÇAL HORS D'OEUVRE

Tuna Fish Salad

1 (99-g/3½-oz) can tuna fish, drained
  and flaked
1 hard-boiled egg, thinly sliced
2 small spring onions, sliced
1 teaspoon finely chopped parsley
4 tablespoons French Dressing (page 159)

1. Arrange flaked tuna fish in an hors d'oeuvre dish.

2. Top tuna fish with thinly sliced hard-boiled egg, scatter with sliced spring onions and sprinkle with finely chopped parsley. Pour over French Dressing and serve.

Serves 4

Ratatouille Salad

1 (390-g/13.8-oz) can ratatouille
1 (213-g/7½-oz) can button mushrooms,
  drained and thinly sliced
½ clove garlic, finely chopped
2 teaspoons finely chopped parsley
2 teaspoons capers
1 tablespoon finely chopped onion
6 anchovy fillets, cut into thin strips
6 black olives, stoned

1. Empty contents of ratatouille can into an hors d'oeuvre dish.

2. Add thinly sliced mushrooms, finely chopped garlic and parsley, and capers. Scatter with finely chopped onion. Garnish with a lattice of anchovy strips dotted with black olives and serve.

Serves 4

Tomato Salad

4–6 ripe tomatoes, chilled
150 ml/¼ pint French Dressing (page 159)
½ small onion, thinly sliced into rings and
  soaked in iced water
3 spring onions, thinly sliced

1. Cut tomatoes crossways into even-sized slices and arrange in a salad bowl or on four individual serving plates.

2. Pour French Dressing over tomatoes, scatter with thinly sliced onion rings and spring onion and serve.

Serves 4

VARIATION

A Add 4 to 6 diced anchovy fillets, 1 coarsely chopped clove garlic and 1 tablespoon coarsely chopped parsley to French Dressing before pouring it over tomatoes.

Elegant Shellfish and Citrus Cocktail

24 cooked prawns
18 small oysters, shelled and chilled
450 g/1 lb cooked lobster meat, cut into
  12–18 even-sized slices
3 oranges, chilled
150 ml/¼ pint mayonnaise
Tabasco sauce
lemon juice
12–18 lettuce leaves

1.   Peel oranges and cut away all white pith. Slip knife blade between each segment and membrane and cut segment out. Remove any pips.

2.   Reserve 6 prawns for garnish and peel remainder.

3.   Season mayonnaise with Tabasco to taste, and moisten with a little lemon juice.

4.   Arrange 2 or 3 lettuce leaves in each of six individual, tulip-shaped glasses. Pile prawns, oysters and orange segments into lettuce-lined glasses and spoon over mayonnaise. Top each glass with 2 or 3 lobster slices, curl a reserved prawn over edge of each glass and serve.

Serves 6

Canned Sardine and Lemon Cocktail

2 (120-g/4¼-oz) cans sardines in oil,
  drained and chilled
juice of ½ lemon
2 tablespoons olive oil
2 tablespoons finely chopped onion
2 tablespoons coarsely chopped flat-
  leafed parsley
8–12 lettuce leaves
1 x recipe quantity cocktail sauce of your
  choice (page 24)
4 thin lemon wedges

1.   Skin and bone sardines and cut into small pieces.

2.   Combine lemon juice, olive oil, finely chopped onion and coarsely chopped parsley in a porcelain or earthenware (not metal) bowl. Add sardine pieces and marinate for 15 minutes. Drain.

3.   Arrange 2 or 3 lettuce leaves in each of four individual cocktail glasses. Pile sardine pieces into lettuce-lined glasses. Pour over cocktail sauce of your choice, garnish with lemon wedges and serve.

Serves 4

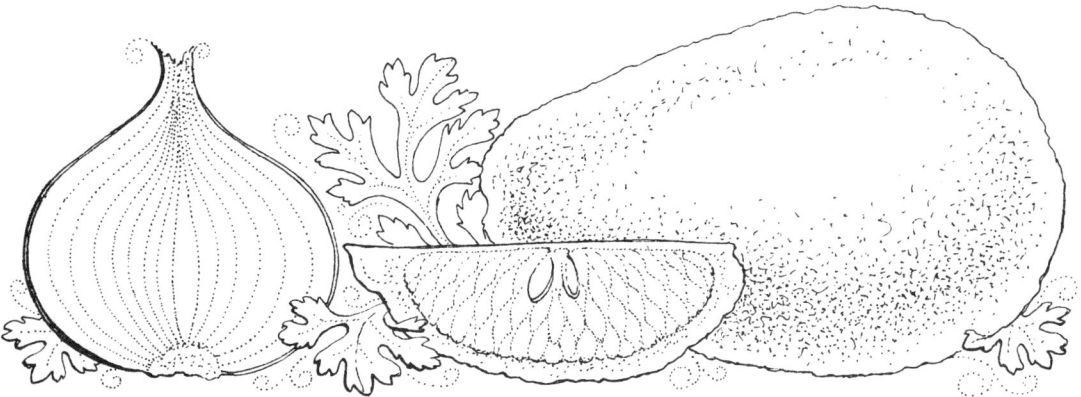

Seafood and Avocado Cocktail

1 (100-g/4-oz) can lobster meat, drained and diced
1 (198-g/7-oz) can shrimps, drained and diced
100 g/4 oz cooked prawns, peeled
1 large ripe avocado pear
lemon juice
4 tablespoons olive oil
salt and freshly ground black pepper
8–12 lettuce leaves
1 x recipe quantity Horseradish Cocktail Sauce or American Cocktail Sauce (page 24)
2 tablespoons finely chopped chives or parsley
4 lemon wedges

1. Cut avocado pear in half, remove stone and peel avocado. Cut into even dice and sprinkle with lemon juice to preserve colour.

2. Combine 4 tablespoons lemon juice and the olive oil, and season to taste with salt and freshly ground black pepper. Add diced avocado and toss thoroughly.

3. Add diced lobster meat and the shrimps and prawns to avocado and toss again. Chill.

4. Arrange 2 or 3 lettuce leaves in each of four individual cocktail glasses. Pile avocado and seafood mixture into each lettuce-lined glass and pour over Horseradish Cocktail Sauce or American Cocktail Sauce. Sprinkle with finely chopped chives or parsley, garnish with lemon wedges and serve.

Serves 4

Mexican Seviche of Salmon or Scallops

450 g/1 lb salmon fillets, or 350 g/12 oz shelled scallops
3 tablespoons lemon juice
3 tablespoons lime juice
150 ml/$\frac{1}{4}$ pint olive oil
4 tablespoons finely chopped onion
1 clove garlic, finely chopped
finely chopped parsley or coriander leaves
dash of Tabasco sauce or Worcestershire sauce
salt and freshly ground black pepper

1. Cut salmon fillets across the grain into thin strips, or trim scallops and slice horizontally into three even-sized slices. Place salmon strips or scallop slices in a porcelain or earthenware (not metal) bowl. Pour over lemon and lime juice and marinate for 15 minutes.

2. Meanwhile, combine olive oil, finely chopped onion and garlic, and 1 tablespoon finely chopped parsley or coriander leaves in a serving bowl. Season with Tabasco or Worcestershire sauce, and salt and freshly ground black pepper to taste.

3. Drain salmon strips or scallop slices and add to serving bowl. Toss until all ingredients glisten. Sprinkle with finely chopped parsley or coriander leaves and serve.

Serves 4 to 6

Scallops with Saffron Rolf Widmer

8 shelled scallops, with 4 bottom shells
$\frac{1}{4}$ teaspoon saffron strands
4 tablespoons gin
4 tablespoons lemon juice
100 g/4 oz bean sprouts
4 tablespoons dry white wine
6 tablespoons mayonnaise
2 tablespoons chopped chives
4 lettuce cups
4 sprigs fresh coriander or fennel
8 carrot 'flowers', or 4 tomato 'roses'

1. Wash scallops and remove beards. Dry scallops carefully. Reserve corals for garnish. Starting at the outside edge, cut scallops into very thin slices.

2. Combine scallop slices, gin, lemon juice and saffron strands and toss carefully. Chill.

3. Meanwhile, wash and trim bean sprouts. Chill.

4. Bring 4 tablespoons water and the dry white wine to the boil. Pour over corals to 'cook' them. Drain and chill.

5. Wash scallop shells and place on four individual serving plates.

6. Drain scallop slices. Stir gin and saffron marinade into mayonnaise, together with chopped chives.

7. Arrange scallop slices in shells and garnish each shell with 2 'cooked' corals.

8. Toss bean sprouts in flavoured mayonnaise and pile into lettuce cups. Garnish each plate with a lettuce cup, a sprig of coriander or fennel, and 2 carrot 'flowers' or a tomato 'rose' and serve.

Serves 4

Horseradish Cocktail Sauce

1 teaspoon prepared horseradish
150 ml/$\frac{1}{4}$ pint mayonnaise
2 tablespoons lemon juice
2 tablespoons tomato ketchup
4 drops Worcestershire sauce
2 drops Tabasco sauce
salt and freshly ground white pepper

Combine first six ingredients and season to taste with salt and freshly ground white pepper. Chill before serving.

Makes 150–300 ml/$\frac{1}{4}$–$\frac{1}{2}$ pint

American Cocktail Sauce

150 ml/$\frac{1}{4}$ pint tomato ketchup
2 tablespoons soured cream
2 teaspoons finely grated onion
3 tablespoons lemon juice
1 tablespoon Worcestershire sauce
1 teaspoon prepared horseradish
few drops Tabasco sauce
salt

Combine first six ingredients and season to taste with Tabasco and salt. Chill before serving.

Makes 150–300 ml/$\frac{1}{4}$–$\frac{1}{2}$ pint

Scallops with Saffron Rolf Widmer

Provençal Seafood Salad

2 (50-g/2-oz) cooked sole fillets, diced
100 g/4 oz cooked crabmeat, flaked
100 g/4 oz cooked prawns, peeled
2 tablespoons finely chopped shallot
2 tomatoes, peeled, deseeded and cut into
  thin strips
2 tablespoons chopped chives or spring
  onion tops
50 g/2 oz button mushrooms, thinly sliced
8 black olives, stoned
4 sprigs fresh herbs
4 lemon twists

DRESSING
1 tablespoon red wine vinegar
1 tablespoon lemon juice
$\frac{1}{4}$ teaspoon ground saffron
6 tablespoons olive oil
salt and freshly ground black pepper
cayenne

1. To make the dressing, heat red wine vinegar and lemon juice, stir in ground saffron, then stir into olive oil. Beat until mixture thickens and emulsifies. Season to taste with salt, freshly ground black pepper and cayenne.

2. Place diced sole in a small bowl. Add finely chopped shallot and tomato strips.

3. Place flaked crabmeat in another bowl. Add chopped chives or spring onion tops.

4. Place prawns in a third bowl. Add thinly sliced mushrooms.

5. Divide dressing between the three bowls and toss until all ingredients glisten. Place a small pile of each fish on each of four individual serving plates. Garnish with black olives, sprigs of fresh herbs and lemon twists, and serve.

Serves 4

Chicken Salad with Avocado

450 g/1 lb cooked chicken, cut into
  5-mm/$\frac{1}{4}$-in dice
3 large ripe avocado pears
4 tablespoons lemon juice
salt and freshly ground black pepper
4 sticks celery, finely diced
2 oranges, peeled, segmented and diced
150 ml/$\frac{1}{4}$ pint mayonnaise
4 tablespoons tomato ketchup
$\frac{1}{4}$ teaspoon paprika
$\frac{1}{4}$ teaspoon cayenne
3 canned pimientos, finely diced
1 large orange, peeled and segmented
lettuce leaves

1. Cut avocado pears in half and remove stones. Sprinkle avocados with lemon juice to preserve colour and season generously with salt and freshly ground black pepper.

2. Combine diced chicken, finely diced celery and diced oranges.

3. Combine mayonnaise and tomato ketchup and season with paprika, cayenne, and salt and freshly ground black pepper to taste. Fold in chicken mixture. Fill cavities of avocado pears with chicken salad; top with finely diced pimiento and garnish with orange segments. Serve salad on a bed of lettuce leaves.

Serves 6

Chilled Sauerkraut Appetiser Salad

1 (450-g/1-lb) can sauerkraut, drained
3 large radishes, thinly sliced
1 medium-sized green pepper, deseeded
  and thinly sliced
1 cooking apple (unpeeled), thinly sliced
4 tablespoons finely chopped onion
4 tablespoons olive oil
4 tablespoons lemon juice
4 tablespoons mayonnaise
4 tablespoons soured cream
salt and freshly ground black pepper
4 large or 8–12 small tomatoes
sprigs of watercress

1. Combine first nine ingredients and season to taste with salt and freshly ground black pepper. Add a little more lemon juice, if desired. Toss until all ingredients glisten. Chill.

2. Cut tomatoes almost through to the base into even-sized wedges. Open wedges gently to form the 'petals' of a flower. Place 1 large tomato 'flower', or 2 or 3 smaller ones, on each of four individual serving plates. Pile sauerkraut salad in the centre of each plate; garnish with sprigs of watercress and serve.

Serves 4

Avocado and Orange Salad

2 large ripe avocado pears
3 oranges, peeled and sliced crossways
1 Spanish onion, thinly sliced
lemon juice
lettuce leaves
sprigs of watercress
1 x recipe quantity Curried Mayonnaise
  (page 70, Curried Hard-Boiled Eggs)

DRESSING
3 tablespoons olive oil
1 tablespoon lemon juice
salt and freshly ground black pepper

1. To make the dressing, combine olive oil and lemon juice, and season to taste with salt and freshly ground black pepper.

2. Toss orange slices and thinly sliced onion in the dressing. Chill.

3. Meanwhile, cut avocado pears in half, remove stones and peel avocados. Cut each half, lengthways, into six slices, and sprinkle with lemon juice to preserve colour.

4. Drain orange and onion slices.

5. Arrange avocado slices on six to eight individual salad plates, on a bed of lettuce leaves, and top with orange and onion slices. Garnish each plate with watercress sprigs and serve with Curried Mayonnaise.

Serves 6 to 8

Blender Taramasalata

1 (198-g/7-oz) jar smoked cod's roe
6 slices white bread, crusts removed
2 tablespoons grated onion
2 small cloves garlic, mashed
3 tablespoons lemon juice
150 ml/¼ pint olive oil
black olives
1 tablespoon finely chopped parsley
hot toast

1.   Place smoked cod's roe in the bowl of an electric blender or food processor.

2.   Soak bread slices in water, gently squeeze almost dry and add to cod's roe.

3.   Add grated onion, mashed garlic and 1 tablespoon lemon juice to cod's roe and blend for 30 seconds, or until smooth. Then blend in olive oil in a thin stream until well incorporated. Blend in remaining lemon juice. Transfer taramasalata to a serving dish or to six (150-ml/¼-pint) ramekins. Chill.

4.   Garnish taramasalata with black olives and finely chopped parsley, and serve with hot toast.

Serves 6

Blender Tuna Pâté with Truffles

2 (198-g/7-oz) cans tuna fish, drained
2 truffles, coarsely chopped
1 tablespoon Madeira
225 g/8 oz butter, melted
4 tablespoons olive oil
1 teaspoon mustard powder
juice of 1 lemon
2 tablespoons cognac
2 tablespoons finely chopped onion
salt and freshly ground black pepper
1 lemon, cut into 6 wedges
fingers of hot toast

1.   Marinate coarsely chopped truffles in Madeira until needed.

2.   Place tuna fish in the bowl of an electric blender or food processor and blend for 30 seconds, or until smooth.

3.   Gradually add melted butter and olive oil to tuna fish, blending in short bursts.

4.   Combine mustard powder and lemon juice and add to tuna fish mixture, together with cognac and finely chopped onion. Blend again. Season with a little salt and a generous amount of freshly ground black pepper. Fold in truffles, together with the Madeira they were marinated in. Transfer to six (150-ml/¼-pint) ramekins. Chill.

5.   Garnish each ramekin with a lemon wedge and serve with fingers of hot toast.

Serves 6

Blender Taramasalata

Curried Sardine Mould

2 (124-g/4⅜-oz) cans sardines in oil,
  drained
100 g/4 oz butter, melted
2 tablespoons double cream
1½ tablespoons finely chopped chives
1 tablespoon curry paste
3 tablespoons lemon juice
¼ teaspoon cayenne
salt and freshly ground black pepper
4–6 stuffed olives, sliced
lemon slices
fingers of hot toast

1. Mash sardines to a smooth paste. Add melted butter. Then add double cream, finely chopped chives, curry paste and lemon juice, and season with cayenne and generous amounts of salt and freshly ground black pepper.

2. Lightly butter six (150-ml/¼-pint) individual moulds and fill with the sardine mixture. Chill.

3. Dip moulds into hot water for 30 seconds and turn out on to six individual serving plates. Garnish tops of moulds with sliced olives, and garnish plates with lemon slices. Serve with fingers of hot toast.

Serves 6

Japanese Rare Beef Salad

16 thin slices very rare roast beef
2 tablespoons olive oil
2 teaspoons sesame oil
lime juice
50 g/2 oz cucumber, peeled and cut into
  thin strips
50 g/2 oz fresh root ginger, peeled and cut
  into thin strips
8–12 button mushrooms, trimmed
bunch of chives, trimmed and cut into
  even-sized lengths

DRESSING
4 tablespoons olive oil
½–¾ teaspoon soy sauce
2 tablespoons lime juice
salt and freshly ground black pepper

1. Combine olive oil, sesame oil, and lime juice to taste. Dip each slice of rare roast beef in this mixture to flavour each side. Fold each slice into a small square and arrange four squares on each of four individual serving plates.

2. Combine cucumber and ginger strips.

3. To make the dressing, combine olive oil, soy sauce and lime juice, and season to taste with salt and freshly ground black pepper.

4. Pour dressing over cucumber and ginger strips and toss until vegetables glisten. Arrange a small pile of vegetables in the centre of each plate. Garnish each plate with mushrooms and chives and serve.

Serves 4

Anchoïade

1 (50-g/1¾-oz) can anchovy fillets,
  drained
1 large clove garlic
1 teaspoon olive oil
1 tablespoon melted butter
1 tablespoon lemon juice or cognac
freshly ground black pepper
3 thick slices day-old French bread

1. Preheat oven to hot (230 C, 450 F, gas 8).

2. Preheat grill to high.

3. Combine anchovy fillets and garlic in a mortar and pound to a smooth paste. Add olive oil, melted butter and lemon juice or cognac, and season to taste with freshly ground black pepper.

4. Cut bread in half lengthways and toast under preheated grill on cut side only.

5. While bread is still hot, spread anchoïade on toasted side, pressing paste well in. Place in preheated oven for a few minutes, or until bubbling. Slice into even-sized finger portions and serve immediately.

Serves 6

Artichoke Hearts with Foie Gras

4 large or 8 small canned artichoke hearts
4 thick or 8 thin slices canned pâté de
  foie gras
lemon juice
olive oil
salt and freshly ground black pepper
150 ml/¼ pint French Dressing (page 159)
8 lettuce leaves
8 tomato wedges
8 black olives, stoned

1. Rinse artichoke hearts in cold water. Drain on absorbent kitchen paper.

2. Sprinkle artichoke hearts with lemon juice and olive oil and season generously with salt and freshly ground black pepper.

3. Place 1 or 2 artichoke hearts on each of four individual serving plates. Spoon over half the French Dressing and garnish each plate with 2 lettuce leaves, 2 tomato wedges and 2 black olives. Place 1 pâté slice on each heart, spoon over remaining dressing and serve.

Serves 4

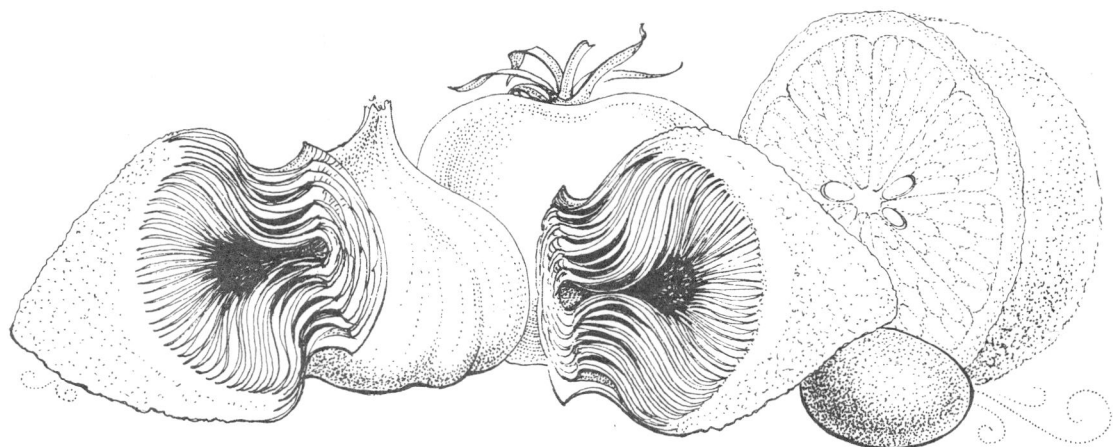

Artichoke Hearts with Seafood and Rouille

4 canned artichoke hearts
lemon juice
olive oil
salt and freshly ground black pepper
8 lettuce leaves, or other salad leaves
8 tomato wedges (optional)
8 black olives, stoned
chopped parsley

SEAFOOD SALAD
450 g/1 lb cooked sole, halibut or turbot
  fillets, chilled
225 g/8 oz cooked prawns, peeled and
  chilled
150 ml/¼ pint French Dressing (page 159)
finely chopped garlic
finely chopped parsley

ROUILLE MAYONNAISE
1 slice white bread, crusts removed
2 large cloves garlic
1 tablespoon paprika
cayenne or crushed hot red peppers
2 tablespoons olive oil
4 tablespoons mayonnaise

1. To prepare Seafood Salad, cut fish fillets into strips. Combine with prawns. Add French Dressing, flavoured to taste with finely chopped garlic and parsley, and toss until all ingredients glisten.

2. To make Rouille Mayonnaise, soak bread slice in water and gently squeeze almost dry. Combine bread, garlic, paprika and a little cayenne or crushed hot red peppers in a mortar and pound until smooth. Gradually add olive oil and mayonnaise and blend to a smooth, aromatic paste.

3. Rinse artichoke hearts in cold water. Drain on absorbent kitchen paper.

4. Sprinkle artichoke hearts with lemon juice and olive oil and season generously with salt and freshly ground black pepper.

5. Place 1 artichoke heart on each of four serving plates. Garnish each with 2 lettuce or other salad leaves, 2 tomato wedges and 2 black olives. Pile Seafood Salad on each heart and top with 2 to 3 tablespoons Rouille Mayonnaise. Sprinkle with a little chopped parsley and serve, with remaining sauce handed separately.

Serves 4

Artichoke Hearts with Seafood and Rouille

Individual Crab Quiches

50 g/2 oz cooked crabmeat, flaked
15 g/$\frac{1}{2}$ oz butter
3 rashers bacon, finely chopped
2 tablespoons finely chopped onion
1 tablespoon finely chopped parsley
4–6 (5-cm/2-in) half baked pastry cases
1 egg, lightly beaten
100 ml/4 fl oz single cream
salt and freshly ground black pepper

1. Preheat oven to moderate (180 C, 350 F, gas 4).

2. Melt butter in a thick-bottomed frying pan and sauté finely chopped bacon until crisp. Remove from pan with a slotted spoon. Sauté finely chopped onion in the same fats until soft but not coloured. Remove from pan with a slotted spoon.

3. Combine bacon, onion, flaked crabmeat and finely chopped parsley, and spoon into half baked pastry cases.

4. Combine lightly beaten egg and single cream, and season to taste with salt and freshly ground black pepper. Pour custard mixture into pastry cases and bake in preheated oven for 15 minutes, or until pastry crusts are golden brown and custard is set. Serve immediately.

Serves 4 to 6

Tapénade Tarts

1 (150-g/5-oz) jar black olives, drained and stoned
1 (50-g/1$\frac{3}{4}$-oz) can anchovy fillets, drained
3 (99-g/3$\frac{1}{2}$-oz) cans tuna fish, drained
1 tablespoon Dijon mustard
3 tablespoons chopped capers
150 ml/$\frac{1}{4}$ pint olive oil
1 tablespoon cognac
2 hard-boiled eggs, sieved
pinch of cayenne
freshly ground black pepper
6 (7.5-cm/3-in) prebaked pastry cases
24 whole black olives
sprigs of basil

1. Combine stoned black olives, anchovy fillets, tuna fish, Dijon mustard and chopped capers in the bowl of an electric blender or food processor. Blend for 4 to 5 minutes, or until a smooth paste forms.

2. Gradually blend olive oil into tapénade mixture. When all the oil has been incorporated, add cognac and sieved hard-boiled egg. Season with cayenne, and freshly ground black pepper to taste.

3. Spoon tapénade into prebaked pastry cases. Garnish with black olives and sprigs of basil and serve.

Serves 6

Tapénade Tarts

CHAPTER THREE

SOUPS

Cold Creamed Asparagus Soup

1 (450-g/1-lb) packet frozen green
 asparagus spears
75 g/3 oz butter
600 ml/1 pint hot chicken stock
salt and freshly ground black pepper
pinch of cayenne (optional)
150 ml/¼ pint double cream

1.   Reserve 8 to 12 asparagus tips for garnish and coarsely chop remaining spears.

2.   Melt butter in a thick-bottomed saucepan and cook coarsely chopped asparagus spears until limp. Transfer to the bowl of an electric blender or food processor and blend to a smooth purée.

3.   Return asparagus purée to pan and add hot chicken stock. Season to taste with salt and freshly ground black pepper, and a pinch of cayenne if desired. Bring to the boil, lower heat and simmer for 5 minutes, or until smooth and well blended.

4.   Add double cream and reserved asparagus tips to pan and continue cooking for a further 5 minutes, or until asparagus tips are just tender. Remove pan from heat. Allow to cool, then chill.

5.   Transfer soup to individual soup bowls, placing 2 or 3 asparagus tips in each bowl, and serve.

Serves 4

Cold Yogurt Soup

600 ml/1 pint natural yogurt
2 medium-sized cucumbers
salt
1 clove garlic, cut
1 tablespoon red wine vinegar
1 teaspoon dill seeds
olive oil
1 tablespoon chopped mint

1.   Peel cucumber, cut lengthways into quarters and cut each quarter into slices 3 mm/⅛ in thick. Place slices in a bowl and sprinkle with salt.

2.   Rub another bowl with cut garlic. Discard garlic and swirl red wine vinegar around bowl to collect flavour. Add dill seeds and natural yogurt and stir until mixture is the consistency of a thick soup, adding cold water if necessary. Pour the mixture over cucumber slices. Stir again.

3.   Transfer soup to eight individual soup bowls. Sprinkle each bowl with a little olive oil, garnish with chopped mint and serve.

Serves 8

Dutch Pea Soup

450 g/1 lb frozen peas
1.15 litres/2 pints chicken stock (made
  with 2 chicken stock cubes)
175 g/6 oz bacon, in one piece
2 sticks celery, finely chopped
1 clove garlic, finely chopped
1 Spanish onion, finely chopped
4 sprigs parsley
bay leaf
$\frac{1}{2}$ teaspoon dried thyme
25 g/1 oz butter
4 frankfurters, thinly sliced
salt and freshly ground black pepper
2 tablespoons finely chopped parsley
1 hard-boiled egg, finely chopped

1. Combine peas, chicken stock, bacon, finely chopped celery and garlic, three-quarters of the finely chopped onion, sprigs of parsley, bay leaf and dried thyme in a thick-bottomed saucepan. Bring to the boil. Skim, lower heat and simmer for 20 minutes.

2. Meanwhile, melt butter in a thick-bottomed frying pan and sauté thinly sliced frankfurters for 2 to 3 minutes, or until golden brown. Keep warm.

3. Remove parsley sprigs, bay leaf and bacon from pan. Discard parsley sprigs and bay leaf, and dice bacon.

4. Pour soup into the bowl of an electric blender or food processor and blend until smooth. Pass through a fine sieve.

5. Return soup to a clean pan. Add frankfurter and bacon and season to taste with salt and freshly ground black pepper. Heat through.

6. Transfer soup to a heated tureen or six individual bowls. Garnish with finely chopped parsley, hard-boiled egg and remaining onion, and serve immediately.

Serves 6

Quick Blender Bisque

200 g/7 oz cooked white fish, flaked
450 ml/$\frac{3}{4}$ pint milk
1 tablespoon flour
25 g/1 oz butter
1 small stick celery, diced
1 thin slice onion
salt and freshly ground black pepper

1. Combine first six ingredients in the container of an electric blender or food processor, and blend until smooth. Season to taste with salt and freshly ground black pepper.

2. Pour fish mixture into a thick-bottomed saucepan and bring just to the boil, stirring occasionally.

3. Transfer bisque to a heated soup tureen, or to three individual heated soup bowls, and serve immediately.

Serves 3

VARIATIONS

Lobster Bisque

Cook as in basic recipe (above), substituting 1 (100-g/4-oz) can lobster meat, drained, for flaked white fish, and adding $\frac{1}{2}$ teaspoon tomato purée and 1 teaspoon cognac with the seasonings.

Crab Bisque

Cook as in basic recipe (above), substituting 1 (169-g/6-oz) can crabmeat, drained, for flaked white fish.

Oyster and Spinach Soup with Caviar

16 opened oysters, on the half shell
75 g/3 oz spinach leaves (see note below)
1 (50-g/2-oz) jar red caviar
65 g/2½ oz butter
1 Spanish onion, coarsely chopped
1 stick celery, coarsely chopped
1 small carrot, coarsely chopped
4 sprigs parsley, coarsely chopped
4 tablespoons flour
900 ml/1½ pints hot fish stock
2 tablespoons dry white wine
350 ml/12 fl oz double cream
lemon juice
salt and freshly ground black pepper

1. Melt 50 g/2 oz butter in a thick-bottomed saucepan and sauté coarsely chopped onion, celery, carrot and parsley until vegetables are soft but not coloured.

2. Add flour to pan and cook for 2 to 3 minutes, stirring constantly, until flour is cooked through. Add hot fish stock and simmer until smooth and well blended.

3. Meanwhile, prepare oysters. Using the point of a sharp knife, remove oysters from shells over a thick-bottomed saucepan to catch any juices. Add oysters to pan, together with dry white wine. Cover and simmer for 1 minute. Remove oysters from pan with a slotted spoon and keep warm. Reserve cooking liquid.

4. Prepare spinach parcels. Wash spinach leaves several times in cold water and drain. Remove coarse stems and any damaged or yellowed leaves. Sauté spinach in remaining butter. Make eight parcels the size of the oysters. Keep warm.

5. Prepare cream and caviar garnish. Whip 6 tablespoons double cream until stiff. Season with a squeeze of lemon juice, and salt and freshly ground black pepper to taste. Place 1 teaspoon whipped cream in each oyster half shell and garnish with a little red caviar.

6. To finish soup, add remaining double cream to soup and bring just to the boil. Add reserved liquid oysters were cooked in. Pass soup through a fine sieve. Correct seasoning.

7. Place 2 poached oysters in each of eight heated soup bowls. Pour over soup and place one spinach parcel in the centre of each bowl. Serve immediately, with oyster shell garnish handed separately.

Serves 8

Note If you like, increase the quantity of spinach and make extra parcels for the garnish.

Oyster and Spinach Soup with Caviar

Consommé with Port

750 ml/1¼ pints Quick Beef Consommé
  (page 48)
4 tablespoons port
1 x recipe quantity Individual French
  Omelette (page 64), cut into thin strips

1. Pour consommé into a thick-bottomed saucepan and bring to the boil. Add port.

2. Transfer consommé to individual heated soup bowls. Garnish each bowl with thin strips of omelette and serve immediately.

Serves 4

Consommé with Chinese Won Tons

1 x recipe quantity Quick Chicken
  Consommé (page 48)
salt
2 tablespoons chopped spring onion
soy sauce

DOUGH
75 g/3 oz flour
½ teaspoon salt
1 egg, lightly beaten

FILLING
225 g/8 oz cooked pork, finely minced
1 egg, beaten
½ teaspoon soy sauce
salt and freshly ground black pepper

1. To make the dough, sift flour and salt into a mixing bowl. Stir in lightly beaten egg. Gradually add 3 tablespoons water, mixing constantly. Turn out on to a floured board and knead until smooth. Cover and allow to stand for 10 minutes.

2. Meanwhile, combine filling ingredients.

3. Roll out dough as thinly as possible and cut into 7.5-cm/3-in squares. Place 1 teaspoon filling in the centre of each square. Fold squares in half diagonally to form triangles and press edges together with the tines of a fork.

4. Drop won tons into about 1 litre/2 pints boiling salted water and cook for 15 minutes, or until won tons float to the surface. Remove from pan with a slotted spoon. Drain on absorbent kitchen paper.

5. Meanwhile, heat Quick Chicken Consommé through.

6. Place 4 won tons in each of six individual heated soup bowls and sprinkle with chopped spring onion. Season each bowl with a little soy sauce, pour over consommé and serve immediately.

Serves 6

My Bouillabaisse

4 (50-g/2-oz) huss (rock salmon) steaks
4 (50-g/2-oz) sea bass or red mullet
  steaks
4 (50-g/2-oz) gurnard or monkfish steaks
4 (50-g/2-oz) conger eel steaks
8 slices peeled potato
$\frac{1}{4}$ teaspoon saffron strands
$\frac{1}{2}$ chicken stock cube, crumbled
1 tablespoon olive oil
1 medium-sized Spanish onion, finely
  chopped
1 fat clove garlic, finely chopped
3 canned peeled Italian tomatoes, halved,
  deseeded and chopped
1 tablespoon tomato purée
$\frac{1}{4}$ teaspoon ground turmeric
450 ml/$\frac{3}{4}$ pint Quick Fish Stock (page
  48)
bouquet garni (1 stick celery with leaves,
  sprig of parsley, small bay leaf, 1 stick
  fennel, sprig of tarragon, 12 black
  peppercorns)
4 cooked prawns
8 cooked mussels, in half shells

ROBERT CARRIER'S DRY MARINADE
$\frac{1}{2}$ chicken stock cube, crumbled
2 teaspoons lemon juice
$\frac{1}{4}$ teaspoon cayenne

1.   Ask your fishmonger to cut small, even-sized steaks from the tail ends of fish—huss, sea bass or red mullet, gurnard or monkfish, and conger eel. Place fish steaks in a shallow dish large enough to take them in one layer.

2.   Combine dry marinade ingredients and sprinkle over steaks. Allow to stand for 5 minutes, then turn steaks over so that they are thoroughly impregnated with marinade flavours and allow to stand for a further 5 minutes.

3.   Meanwhile, place potato slices in a thick-bottomed saucepan and pour over 150 ml/$\frac{3}{4}$ pint water. Add saffron strands and crumbled $\frac{1}{2}$ chicken stock cube. Bring to the boil, reduce heat and cook until potato slices are tender, then drain.

4.   Heat olive oil in a thick-bottomed frying pan and sauté finely chopped onion and garlic until vegetables are soft but not coloured. Add chopped tomatoes, tomato purée, turmeric, Quick Fish Stock and bouquet garni, and bring to the boil. Add fish steaks and continue to cook over a high heat, skimming from time to time, until stock begins to boil again. Reduce heat, add cooked prawns and mussels, and saffron-flavoured potato slices, and simmer until heated through. Discard bouquet garni.

5.   Transfer bouillabaisse to a heated soup tureen, or to four individual soup bowls, and serve immediately.

Serves 4

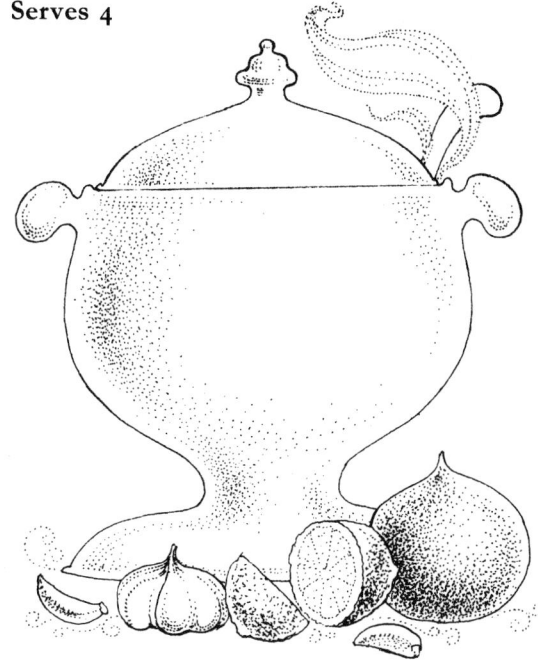

Prawn and Corn Chowder

100 g/4 oz frozen Norwegian prawns,
  defrosted
1 (340-g/12-oz) can sweet corn, drained
15 g/½ oz butter
1 tablespoon flour
600 ml/1 pint hot chicken stock
1 canned red pimiento, cut into thin
  strips
1–2 tablespoons lemon juice
1–2 teaspoons soy sauce
freshly ground black pepper
cayenne
chopped coriander

1.   Melt butter in a thick-bottomed saucepan, add flour and cook for 2 to 3 minutes, stirring constantly, until flour is cooked through. Gradually add hot chicken stock and cook, stirring vigorously, until smooth and well blended.

2.   Add prawns, sweet corn and pimiento strips to pan, and season with lemon juice, soy sauce, and freshly ground black pepper and cayenne to taste. Bring to the boil.

3.   Transfer chowder to a heated soup tureen, or to four individual heated soup bowls, garnish with a little chopped coriander and serve immediately.

Serves 4

Creamed Mushroom Soup

225 g/8 oz button mushrooms
50 g/2 oz butter
3 tablespoons flour
750 ml/1¼ pints hot chicken stock
juice of ½ lemon
150 ml/¼ pint double cream
2 tablespoons chopped parsley
salt and freshly ground black pepper
freshly grated nutmeg

1.   Wipe mushrooms clean with a damp cloth and trim stems. Thinly slice half and finely chop remainder.

2.   Melt butter in a thick-bottomed saucepan, add flour and cook for 2 to 3 minutes, stirring constantly, until flour is cooked through. Gradually add hot chicken stock and bring to the boil, stirring vigorously.

3.   Add sliced mushrooms and lemon juice to pan and cook for 5 minutes. Pour soup into the bowl of an electric blender or food processor, and blend until smooth. Pass through a fine sieve.

4.   Return soup to a clean pan. Add double cream, chopped parsley and finely chopped mushrooms, and season to taste with salt, freshly ground black pepper and freshly grated nutmeg. Heat through.

5.   Transfer soup to a heated soup tureen, or to four individual soup bowls, and serve immediately.

Serves 4

Prawn and Corn Chowder

Green Gazpacho

4 ripe avocado pears
lemon juice
1.75 litres/3 pints chilled chicken stock
salt and freshly ground white pepper
6 drops Tabasco sauce
150 ml/$\frac{1}{4}$ pint double cream
2 tomatoes, peeled, deseeded and
  coarsely chopped
2 rashers bacon, cooked and diced
$\frac{1}{4}$ cucumber, peeled and diced
1–2 tablespoons finely chopped parsley

1. Cut avocado pears in half, remove stones and peel avocados. Sprinkle flesh with lemon juice to preserve colour. Cut 1 avocado half into small dice. Reserve.

2. Purée remaining avocado halves with chilled chicken stock in an electric blender or food processor. Season to taste with salt and freshly ground white pepper. Add Tabasco and double cream. Correct seasoning.

3. Transfer soup to a soup tureen and stir in reserved diced avocado. Chill.

4. Serve soup, with chopped tomatoes, diced bacon and cucumber, and finely chopped parsley as separate accompaniments. Guests help themselves.

Serves 8

Jellied Gazpacho

6 large ripe tomatoes, peeled, deseeded
  and coarsely diced
1 medium-sized onion, finely chopped
1 clove garlic, finely chopped
1 medium-sized green pepper, deseeded
  and thinly sliced
$\frac{1}{2}$ cucumber, peeled and thinly sliced
dash of Tabasco sauce
salt and freshly ground black pepper
4 tablespoons olive oil
2 tablespoons white wine vinegar
2 (425-g/15-oz) cans jellied chicken
  consommé, chilled
1 tablespoon finely chopped parsley
lemon wedges

1. Combine coarsely diced tomatoes, finely chopped onion and garlic, and thinly sliced green pepper and cucumber in a porcelain or earthenware (not metal) bowl. Season with Tabasco and salt and freshly ground black pepper to taste. Pour over olive oil and white wine vinegar and marinate in the refrigerator for 15 to 20 minutes.

2. Fold chilled jellied chicken consommé and finely chopped parsley into soup.

3. Transfer soup to a soup tureen, or to four individual soup bowls, and serve, accompanied by lemon wedges.

Serves 4

Thai Chicken Soup

275 g/10 oz chicken meat, minced with a
  little salt
900 ml/1½ pints boiling chicken stock
  (made with 1 chicken stock cube)
6 button mushrooms, quartered
1 stick celery, thinly sliced
¼ teaspoon finely chopped fresh root
  ginger
1–3 teaspoons Thai fish sauce
freshly ground black pepper
6 lettuce leaves, shredded
2 spring onions, chopped

1. Form minced chicken meat into 12 small
balls. Drop into boiling chicken stock, lower
heat and simmer for 5 minutes.

2. Add quartered mushrooms, thinly sliced
celery, finely chopped ginger and Thai fish
sauce to pan, and season to taste with freshly
ground black pepper. Add shredded lettuce
and chopped spring onions and cook for a
further 2 minutes.

3. Transfer soup to a heated soup tureen, or
to individual heated soup bowls, and serve
immediately.

Serves 4 to 6

Thai Prawn Soup

275 g/10 oz cooked prawns, peeled and
  minced
900 ml/1½ pints boiling chicken stock
  (made with 1 chicken stock cube)
¼ teaspoon finely chopped fresh root
  ginger
1–3 teaspoons Thai fish sauce
freshly ground black pepper
6 lettuce leaves, shredded
2 spring onions, chopped
2 tablespoons chopped coriander leaves
1–2 tablespoons lemon juice
½–1 teaspoon sugar

1. Form minced prawns into 12 small balls.
Drop into boiling chicken stock, lower heat
and simmer for 5 minutes.

2. Add finely chopped ginger and Thai fish
sauce to pan and season to taste with freshly
ground black pepper. Add shredded lettuce
and chopped spring onions and coriander
leaves and cook for a further 2 minutes. Add
lemon juice and sugar to taste.

3. Transfer soup to a heated soup tureen, or
to individual heated soup bowls, and serve
immediately.

Serves 4 to 6

CHAPTER FOUR

SAUCES

Quick Chicken Stock

100 g/4 oz chicken meat, minced
10 black peppercorns, crushed
½ bay leaf
pinch of dried thyme
1 stick celery, finely chopped
½ small carrot, finely chopped
1 tablespoon finely chopped mushroom
  stalks or peelings
½ leek, roughly chopped
3 parsley stalks

1. Place minced chicken meat in a thick-bottomed saucepan and cover with 1.75 litres/3 pints water.

2. Add to the pan crushed black peppercorns, ½ bay leaf, dried thyme, finely chopped celery, carrot and mushroom stalks or peelings, roughly chopped leek, and parsley stalks; bring to the boil. Reduce heat and simmer for 20 to 25 minutes. Strain through a fine sieve.

Makes 600–750 ml/1–1¼ pints

Quick Beef Stock

100 g/4 oz lean beef, minced
10 black peppercorns, crushed
½ bay leaf
pinch of dried thyme
1 stick celery, finely chopped
½ small carrot, finely chopped
1 tablespoon finely chopped mushroom
  stalks or peelings
½ leek, roughly chopped
3 parsley stalks

1. Place minced beef in a thick-bottomed saucepan and cover with 1.75 litres/3 pints water.

2. Add to the pan crushed black peppercorns, ½ bay leaf, dried thyme, finely chopped celery, carrot and mushroom stalks or peelings, roughly chopped leek, and parsley stalks; bring to the boil. Reduce heat and simmer for 20 to 25 minutes. Strain through a fine sieve.

Makes 600–750 ml/1–1¼ pints

*Home-made stocks and glaces contribute
immeasurably to your finished dish*

Quick Fish Stock

**225 g/8 oz bones and trimmings from
  sole, plaice or turbot
1 stick celery, finely chopped
½ leek, finely chopped
1 medium-sized onion, finely chopped
½ bay leaf
3 white peppercorns, crushed
2 parsley stalks**

1. Place fish bones and trimmings in a thick-bottomed saucepan and cover with 1.15 litres/2 pints water.

2. Add to the pan finely chopped celery, leek and onion, ½ bay leaf, crushed white peppercorns, and parsley stalks; bring to the boil. Reduce heat and simmer for 20 to 25 minutes. Strain through a fine sieve.

Makes 600–750 ml/1–1¼ pints

Quick Chicken Consommé

**2 (425-g/15-oz) cans chicken consommé
75 g/3 oz chicken meat, minced
½ small carrot, finely chopped
1 stick celery, finely chopped
1 small onion, finely chopped
½ leek, finely chopped
2 over-ripe tomatoes, roughly squeezed
2 parsley stalks
pinch of dried thyme
½ bay leaf, crushed
1 teaspoon tomato purée
salt and freshly ground black pepper**

1. Empty contents of chicken consommé cans into a thick-bottomed saucepan.

2. Add to the pan 1.15 litres/2 pints water, minced chicken meat, finely chopped carrot, celery, onion and leek, roughly squeezed tomatoes, parsley stalks, dried thyme, crushed ½ bay leaf, and tomato purée. Season to taste with salt and freshly ground black pepper. Bring to the boil, reduce heat and simmer for 20 to 25 minutes. Strain through a fine sieve.

Makes 1.4 litres/2½ pints

Quick Beef Consommé

**2 (425-g/15-oz) cans beef consommé
75 g/3 oz lean beef, minced
½ small carrot, finely chopped
1 stick celery, finely chopped
1 small onion, finely chopped
½ leek, finely chopped
2 over-ripe tomatoes, roughly squeezed
2 parsley stalks
pinch of dried thyme
½ bay leaf, crushed
1 teaspoon tomato purée
salt and freshly ground black pepper**

1. Empty contents of beef consommé cans into a thick-bottomed saucepan.

2. Add to the pan 1.15 litres/2 pints water, minced beef, finely chopped carrot, celery, onion and leek, roughly squeezed tomatoes, parsley stalks, dried thyme, crushed ½ bay leaf, and tomato purée. Season to taste with salt and freshly ground black pepper. Bring to the boil, reduce heat and simmer for 20 to 25 minutes. Strain through a fine sieve.

Makes 1.4 litres/2½ pints

Quick White Sauce

40 g/1½ oz butter
2 tablespoons finely chopped onion
1 rasher bacon, chopped
2 tablespoons flour
150 ml/¼ pint hot chicken stock
450 ml/¾ pint hot milk
1 clove
½ bay leaf
3 white peppercorns, crushed
freshly grated nutmeg

1. Melt butter in a thick-bottomed saucepan and sauté finely chopped onion until soft but not coloured. Add chopped bacon and continue cooking until bacon is golden brown.

2. Add flour to pan and cook for 2 to 3 minutes, stirring constantly, until flour is cooked through. Gradually add hot chicken stock, stirring vigorously. Add hot milk, clove, ½ bay leaf, crushed white peppercorns, and freshly grated nutmeg to taste. Bring to the boil, reduce heat and simmer for 15 minutes, or until sauce is thick and creamy. Strain through a fine sieve.

Makes 300 ml/½ pint

VARIATIONS

Cream Sauce

For fish, poultry, eggs and vegetables. Add 2 tablespoons double cream to hot Quick White Sauce (left) and bring to the boil. Season to taste with lemon juice.

Aurore Sauce

For eggs, chicken and shellfish. Add 1 to 2 tablespoons tomato purée to hot Quick White Sauce (left).

Curry Sauce

For fish, poultry, eggs and vegetables. Add 1 tablespoon curry powder and ½ peeled, cored and diced cooking apple to hot Quick White Sauce (left). Cook, stirring constantly, until sauce just reaches boiling point.

Quick Brown Sauce

40 g/1½ oz butter
1 small onion, thinly sliced
1 teaspoon sugar
3 tablespoons flour
1 (283-g/10-oz) can beef consommé
1 small carrot, thinly sliced
1 stick celery, thinly sliced, or ¼ teaspoon
  celery seeds
4 button mushrooms, thinly sliced
1 tablespoon tomato purée
bouquet garni (3 sprigs parsley, sprig of
  thyme, bay leaf)
1 clove
freshly ground black pepper

1. Brown butter in a thick-bottomed saucepan. Add thinly sliced onion and sugar and simmer, stirring constantly, until onion is golden brown. Stir in flour and continue to simmer, stirring constantly, until flour takes on a brown colour. (The good colour of your sauce depends on the thorough browning of these ingredients without allowing them to burn.)

2. Remove pan from heat and pour in beef consommé. Return pan to heat and cook, stirring constantly, until sauce comes to the boil. Allow to boil for 5 minutes, skimming from time to time. Reduce heat.

3. Add to the pan thinly sliced carrot, celery (or celery seeds) and mushrooms, tomato purée, bouquet garni and clove. Season to taste with freshly ground black pepper. Simmer sauce for 15 minutes, stirring occasionally and skimming from time to time. Strain through a fine sieve.

Makes 300 ml/½ pint

VARIATIONS

Madeira Sauce

For beef fillet, game and gammon. Reduce 600 ml/1 pint Quick Brown Sauce (left) to half the original quantity. Add 6 tablespoons Madeira and heat through; do not allow sauce to come to the boil or the flavour of the Madeira will be lost.

Lyonnaise Sauce

For lamb and vegetables. Sauté 1 finely chopped Spanish onion in 25 g/1 oz butter until golden brown. Add 175 ml/6 fl oz dry white wine and simmer until reduced to half the original quantity. Add hot Quick Brown Sauce (left) and continue cooking for a further 15 minutes. Add 2 teaspoons chopped parsley and 'finish' by swirling in 15 g/½ oz butter.

Demi-Glace Sauce

For baked ham, fillet of beef and saddle of lamb. Simmer the chopped stems and peelings of 6 button mushrooms in 6 tablespoons dry sherry until liquid is reduced by half. Meanwhile, reduce 600 ml/1 pint Quick Brown Sauce (left) by half. Add 1 to 2 tablespoons meat glaze (a reduction of canned beef consommé), and mushroom trimmings together with pan juices, and simmer for 15 minutes. Strain through a fine sieve.

Home-made sauces keep warm over barely simmering water

Béchamel Sauce

butter
2 tablespoons finely chopped onion
2 tablespoons finely chopped ham, veal
  or chicken
$\frac{1}{4}$ chicken stock cube
2 tablespoons flour
450 ml/$\frac{3}{4}$ pint hot milk
$\frac{1}{2}$ bay leaf
6 white peppercorns, crushed
freshly grated nutmeg

1.   Melt 40 g/1$\frac{1}{2}$ oz butter in a thick-bottomed saucepan and sauté finely chopped onion until soft but not coloured. Add finely chopped ham, veal or chicken, $\frac{1}{4}$ chicken stock cube and flour, and cook for 2 to 3 minutes, stirring constantly, until flour is cooked through. Add one-third of the hot milk and cook, stirring vigorously. As sauce begins to thicken, gradually add remaining milk, stirring constantly until sauce begins to bubble.

2.   Remove pan from heat and add $\frac{1}{2}$ bay leaf, crushed white peppercorns, and freshly grated nutmeg to taste. Simmer until sauce has reduced to 300 ml/$\frac{1}{2}$ pint and is thick and smooth. Strain through a fine sieve. Dot surface with a little extra butter.

Makes 300 ml/$\frac{1}{2}$ pint

Note for flavour balance   Boil 4 tablespoons dry white wine until reduced to 1 tablespoon and stir into sauce. Boil 4 tablespoons chicken stock until reduced to 1 tablespoon and stir into sauce. Taste sauce, and if it needs pointing up, add a little salt and freshly ground white pepper, and a squeeze of lemon juice and/or a drop of Tabasco. If flavour seems sharp or strong, soften with a teaspoon or two of Madeira or brandy, and a pinch of sugar. See The Flavour Piano (page 9) for more flavour additives.

VARIATIONS

Mornay Sauce

For fish, vegetables, poultry, poached eggs, noodles and macaroni. Mix 1 lightly beaten egg yolk with a little double cream and combine with hot Béchamel Sauce (left). Cook, stirring constantly, until sauce just reaches boiling point. Add 15 g/$\frac{1}{2}$ oz butter and 2 tablespoons freshly grated Gruyère cheese and continue cooking and stirring until cheese has melted.

Nantua Sauce

For fish and shellfish, and quenelles or mousselines of fish and shellfish. Blend 2 to 4 tablespoons double cream into hot Béchamel Sauce (left). Strain through a fine sieve. Season to taste with salt and freshly ground white pepper. Heat through and stir in 2 tablespoons peeled and diced cooked prawns, shrimps or scampi.

Sauce Soubise

For fish, lamb, veal and sweetbreads. Parboil 1 sliced medium-sized onion. Drain. Sauté in a little butter until soft but not coloured. Add hot Béchamel Sauce (left) and cook for 15 minutes. Strain through a fine sieve. Return to heat. Gradually add 150 ml/$\frac{1}{4}$ pint double cream and season to taste with salt and freshly ground white pepper.

Fish Velouté Sauce

600 ml/1 pint hot Quick Fish Stock (page 48)
25 g/1 oz butter
2 tablespoons flour
pinch of salt
4 white peppercorns, crushed
25 g/1 oz mushroom peelings or chopped stems
2 teaspoons lemon juice

1. Melt butter in a thick-bottomed saucepan. Add flour and cook for 2 to 3 minutes, stirring constantly, until flour is cooked through. Gradually add hot Quick Fish Stock. Season with salt and crushed white peppercorns and cook, stirring vigorously, until smooth and well blended.

2. Add mushroom peelings or chopped stems to sauce. Simmer, stirring occasionally and skimming from time to time, until sauce has reduced to 300 ml/½ pint and is thick, but light and creamy. Flavour with lemon juice. Strain through a fine sieve.

Makes 300 ml/½ pint

Chicken Velouté Sauce

600 ml/1 pint hot chicken stock
25 g/1 oz butter
2 tablespoons flour
pinch of salt
4 white peppercorns, crushed
25 g/1 oz mushroom peelings or chopped stems
2 teaspoons lemon juice

1. Melt butter in a thick-bottomed saucepan, add flour and cook for 2 to 3 minutes, stirring constantly, until flour is cooked through. Gradually add hot chicken stock. Season with salt and crushed white peppercorns and cook, stirring vigorously, until smooth and well blended.

2. Add mushroom peelings or chopped stems to sauce. Simmer, stirring occasionally and skimming from time to time, until sauce has reduced to 300 ml/½ pint and is thick, but light and creamy. Flavour with lemon juice. Strain through a fine sieve.

Makes 300 ml/½ pint

Note This sauce forms the foundation of a number of the best white sauces, which take their distinctive names from the different ingredients added. Chicken Velouté Sauce can be used by itself, but in that case it is much improved by the addition of a little double cream and an egg yolk.

French Tomato Sauce

6–8 ripe tomatoes, sliced
2 tablespoons tomato purée
25 g/1 oz butter
2 tablespoons finely chopped ham
1 small carrot, finely chopped
1 small turnip, finely chopped
1 medium-sized onion, finely chopped
1 stick celery, finely chopped
1 tablespoon flour
bouquet garni (sprig of thyme, sprig of
  parsley, sprig of marjoram)
300 ml/½ pint hot beef stock
salt and freshly ground black pepper
sugar
lemon juice (optional)

1.   Melt butter in a thick-bottomed saucepan and sauté finely chopped ham, carrot, turnip, onion and celery until onion is soft but not coloured.

2.   Add flour and cook for 2 to 3 minutes, stirring constantly, until flour is cooked through. Add sliced tomatoes, tomato purée, bouquet garni and hot beef stock, and season to taste with salt, freshly ground black pepper and sugar. Bring to the boil, reduce heat and simmer for 20 minutes, stirring occasionally. If sauce becomes too thick, add a little more stock. Strain through a fine sieve. Sharpen flavour with lemon juice, if desired.

Makes 300 ml/½ pint

Instant Tomato Sauce

8 tomatoes, peeled, deseeded and cut
  into small dice
2 teaspoons tomato purée
25 g/1 oz butter
4 shallots, finely chopped
1 teaspoon finely chopped basil
300 ml/½ pint dry white wine
salt and freshly ground black pepper

1.   Melt butter in a thick-bottomed saucepan and sauté finely chopped shallots until soft but not coloured.

2.   Add tomato purée, finely chopped basil and dry white wine to pan and simmer until reduced to 300 ml/½ pint. Season to taste with salt and freshly ground black pepper.

3.   Add diced tomatoes to pan and bring to the boil, then remove from heat immediately so diced tomatoes keep their shape.

Makes 300 ml/½ pint

Hot Barbecue Sauce

2 tomatoes, peeled, deseeded and
  chopped
1½ teaspoons tomato ketchup
1 tablespoon red wine vinegar
1 tablespoon Dijon mustard
½ teaspoon salt
freshly ground black pepper

Combine first five ingredients in a thick-bottomed saucepan and season to taste with freshly ground black pepper. Simmer for 15 minutes, or until sauce is thick and smooth.

Makes 150 ml/¼ pint

Hollandaise Sauce

100 g/4 oz unsalted butter
lemon juice
pinch of salt
pinch of white pepper
4 egg yolks

1. Divide butter into four even-sized pieces.

2. Pour 1 teaspoon lemon juice and 1 tablespoon water into the top of a double saucepan and add a pinch each of salt and freshly ground white pepper.

3. Add egg yolks and one-quarter of the butter to pan and stir vigorously and constantly over hot but not boiling water until butter has melted and sauce begins to thicken. Be careful not to allow water over which sauce is cooking to boil at any time.

4. Add second piece of butter to pan and, as butter begins to melt, add third piece, stirring from the bottom of the pan until butter has melted. Add remaining piece of butter, stirring vigorously and constantly until butter has melted.

5. Remove top part of pan from heat and continue to stir for 2 to 3 minutes. Set pan over water again and continue to stir for a further 2 minutes. By this time the emulsion should have formed and your sauce will be thick and creamy.

6. 'Finish' sauce with a few drops of lemon juice. Strain through a fine sieve.

Makes 300 ml/½ pint

Note   If at any time in the operation the sauce should curdle, just throw in an ice cube and beat vigorously to rebind the emulsion.

Béarnaise Sauce

225 g/8 oz unsalted butter
3 sprigs each tarragon and chervil,
  coarsely chopped
1 tablespoon chopped shallots
2 black peppercorns, crushed
2 tablespoons tarragon vinegar
150 ml/¼ pint dry white wine
3 egg yolks
salt
lemon juice
cayenne

1. Divide butter into four even-sized pieces.

2. Combine half the coarsely chopped tarragon and chervil, the chopped shallots, crushed black peppercorns, tarragon vinegar and dry white wine in a thick-bottomed saucepan. Cook over a high heat until liquid is reduced to two-thirds of the original quantity. Strain through a fine sieve and pour into the top of a double saucepan.

3. Beat egg yolks with 1 tablespoon water and add to pan. Stir vigorously and constantly over hot but not boiling water until light and fluffy. Be careful not to allow water over which sauce is cooking to boil at any time.

4. As sauce begins to thicken add one-quarter of the butter, stirring vigorously and constantly until butter has melted.

5. Add second piece of butter to pan and, as butter begins to melt, add third piece, stirring from the bottom of the pan until butter has melted. Add remaining piece of butter, stirring vigorously and constantly until butter has melted. Remove from heat. Season to taste with salt, lemon juice and cayenne. Add remaining tarragon and chervil.

Makes 300 ml/½ pint

Quick Blender Mayonnaise

A simple mayonnaise which can be made in a matter of minutes.

2 egg yolks
2 teaspoons white wine vinegar or lemon juice
½ teaspoon mustard powder
¼ teaspoon salt
freshly ground black pepper
300 ml/½ pint olive oil

1. Combine egg yolks, wine vinegar or lemon juice, mustard powder, salt and 2 tablespoons cold water in the container of an electric blender or food processor. Season to taste with freshly ground black pepper. Blend at moderate speed for 5 seconds, or until smooth.

2. With the motor running at maximum speed, blend in olive oil in a thin stream until well incorporated. Correct seasoning.

Makes 300 ml/½ pint

Note Should mayonnaise show signs of separating, beat in a few drops of hot water to rebind emulsion. Make sure eggs and olive oil are at room temperature.

VARIATIONS

Rémoulade Sauce

For grilled fish, prawns and lobster, and also for cold pork. Add 1 tablespoon finely chopped tarragon, basil or chervil, 1 finely chopped garlic clove, 1 teaspoon mustard powder, 1 teaspoon capers and 2 finely chopped small pickles to Quick Blender Mayonnaise (left).

Tartare Sauce

For grilled and poached fish, and a 'must' for deep-fried mussels, oysters and prawns. Add 1 teaspoon each of chopped parsley, capers, gherkins, tarragon and chervil, and a pinch of sugar, to Quick Blender Mayonnaise (left).

Hot Chocolate Sauce

50 g/2 oz bitter chocolate
175 g/6 oz sugar
2 tablespoons cornflour
pinch of salt
25 g/1 oz butter
2 tablespoons cognac
½ teaspoon finely grated orange rind

1.   Combine sugar, cornflour and salt.

2.   Melt chocolate with 300 ml/½ pint water in a thick-bottomed saucepan. When smooth, add sugar mixture and cook, stirring constantly, until sugar dissolves and sauce is thick. Allow sauce to boil for 3 minutes.

3.   Add butter and cognac to the pan. Remove pan from heat and stir in finely grated orange rind.

Makes 450 ml/¾ pint

VARIATIONS

A   Add 6 tablespoons brandy instead of cognac to Hot Chocolate Sauce (above).

B   Add finely grated rind and juice of 1 orange instead of ½ teaspoon finely grated rind, and 3 tablespoons dark rum instead of cognac, to Hot Chocolate Sauce (above).

Vanilla Custard Sauce

½ teaspoon vanilla essence
450 ml/¾ pint milk
1 tablespoon cornflour
3 tablespoons sugar
4 egg yolks
¼ teaspoon salt

1.   Simmer milk in the top of a double saucepan.

2.   Dissolve cornflour in a little hot milk and add to pan, together with vanilla essence.

3.   Combine sugar, egg yolks and salt and beat until fluffy and lemon-coloured. Blend a little vanilla-flavoured milk into mixture and add to pan. Heat through over hot but not boiling water, stirring constantly, until sauce coats the back of a spoon.

Makes 600 ml/1 pint

Rich Vanilla Sauce

150 ml/¼ pint warm Vanilla Custard
  Sauce (above)
150 ml/¼ pint double cream, whipped
4 tablespoons Grand Marnier

Add whipped cream and Grand marnier to warm Vanilla Custard Sauce.

Makes 300 ml/½ pint

CHAPTER FIVE

Simple Egg Dishes

Hard-Boiled Eggs with Watercress Stuffing

4 hard-boiled eggs
2 tablespoons finely chopped watercress
15 g/½ oz butter, softened
2 teaspoons lemon juice
salt and freshly ground black pepper

1. Cool hard-boiled eggs by plunging them into cold water as soon as they are cooked. Carefully remove shells. Cut eggs to the shape of your choice (page 17) and scoop out yolks.

2. Mash together yolks, softened butter, finely chopped watercress and lemon juice, and season to taste with salt and freshly ground black pepper. Fill egg bases and serve.

Serves 4

Oeufs Mollets

4 eggs
salt
hot buttered toast

1. Slip eggs into boiling water; make sure they are wholly immersed otherwise they will not cook evenly. Reduce heat and cook over barely bubbling water for 5 minutes.

2. Plunge eggs into cold water as soon as they are cooked. Carefully remove shells.

3. Reheat eggs in hot, lightly salted water. Drain on absorbent kitchen paper. Transfer to four individual heated serving plates and serve immediately with hot buttered toast.

Serves 4

VARIATIONS

A   Cook eggs as in basic recipe (left). Serve on a bed of chopped cooked spinach, masked with Hollandaise Sauce (page 55).

B   Cook eggs as in basic recipe (left). Serve in prebaked pastry cases, topped with Instant Tomato Sauce (page 54).

C   Cook eggs as in basic recipe (left) and cool by plunging into cold water. Serve with Sauce Verte, made as follows: whirl 300 ml/½ pint well-flavoured mayonnaise, 4 tablespoons finely chopped watercress and 2 tablespoons finely chopped parsley, tarragon and chervil in an electric blender, or food processor. Season to taste with lemon juice, salt and freshly ground black pepper. **Note** To make a greener-looking sauce a few drops of green food colouring, or a squeeze of chopped cooked spinach, may be added.

Oeufs Mollets with Sauce Verte

Scrambled Eggs

To make scrambled eggs for two people you will need two eggs per person and an extra one for the pan, butter, salt, freshly ground black pepper, double cream, and a little diced butter to whip in at the last minute.

9 large eggs
salt and freshly ground black pepper
butter
4 tablespoons double cream
hot buttered toast

1. Break eggs into a bowl and season to taste with salt and freshly ground black pepper. Mix eggs lightly with a fork—do not beat them.

2. Melt 40 g/1½ oz butter in a thick-bottomed saucepan. When butter is sizzling but not coloured, pour in eggs. Allow them to set slightly and then stir constantly with a wooden spoon, running edge of spoon around pan and drawing eggs into the centre. Cook until eggs are creamy.

3. Whisk double cream and a little diced butter into egg mixture until eggs are fluffy. Transfer to four individual heated serving plates and serve immediately, with hot buttered toast.

Serves 4

VARIATIONS

Scrambled Eggs with Bacon

Add 2 rashers cooked and diced bacon to lightly mixed eggs. Cook as in basic recipe (above) but use bacon fat instead of butter in Step 2.

Cottage Scrambled Eggs

Add 75 ml/3 fl oz milk to lightly mixed eggs. Cook as in basic recipe (left), adding 100 g/4 oz cottage cheese, and paprika to taste, as eggs begin to thicken.

Scrambled Egg 'Rabbit'

Add 75 ml/3 fl oz milk to lightly mixed eggs. Cook as in basic recipe (left), adding 2 teaspoons prepared mustard and 2 tablespoons each cottage cheese and freshly grated Cheddar cheese as eggs begin to thicken. Sprinkle with paprika before serving.

Scrambled Eggs with Smoked Fish

Add 6 tablespoons flaked smoked mackerel, and 1 teaspoon prepared horseradish if desired, to lightly mixed eggs. Cook as in basic recipe (left).

Scrambled Eggs with Green Peppers

Remove seeds from 1 medium-sized green pepper. Parboil green pepper, drain and chop finely. Cook lightly mixed eggs as in basic recipe (left), adding finely chopped pepper as eggs begin to thicken.

Scrambled Eggs with Soured Cream and Spring Onions

Add 4 tablespoons soured cream to lightly mixed eggs. Cook as in basic recipe (left), adding 4 tablespoons chopped spring onion as eggs begin to thicken.

Savoury Scrambled Eggs

Add 1 tablespoon each chopped parsley and chives, and ½ teaspoon grated onion, to lightly mixed eggs. Cook as in basic recipe (left).

Scrambled Eggs Creole

6 eggs
150 ml/$\frac{1}{4}$ pint double cream
$\frac{1}{4}$ teaspoon onion juice
6 tablespoons chopped cooked bacon
  (cooked with $\frac{1}{4}$ crushed garlic clove,
  optional)
2 tablespoons finely chopped canned
  pimiento
1 teaspoon finely chopped chives
salt and freshly ground black pepper
25 g/1 oz butter
6 hot Creole Bread Baskets (below)

1. Break eggs into a bowl. Add double cream, onion juice, chopped cooked bacon and finely chopped pimiento and chives, and season to taste with salt and freshly ground black pepper. Mix eggs lightly with a fork—do not beat them.

2. Melt butter in a thick-bottomed saucepan. Cook eggs as in basic recipe (opposite page).

3. Spoon eggs into hot Creole Bread Baskets and serve immediately.

Serves 6

Creole Bread Baskets

1 large unsliced loaf of bread
4 tablespoons melted butter

1. Preheat grill to high.

2. Cut bread into blocks measuring 5 × 7.5 × 5 cm/2 × 3 × 2 in. Cut centre out of each block, to within 1 cm/$\frac{1}{2}$ in of the bottom, to form baskets.

3. Brush each basket with melted butter and toast under preheated grill until golden brown on all sides.

Makes 6

Scrambled Eggs with Ham and Asparagus

9 eggs
2 tablespoons chopped ham
1 (283-g/10-oz) can asparagus spears,
  chopped
4 tablespoons double cream
salt and freshly ground black pepper
butter
hot toast, or 4 (7.5-cm/3-in) prebaked
  pastry cases (optional)

1. Break eggs into a bowl, add double cream, and season to taste with salt and freshly ground black pepper. Mix eggs lightly with a fork—do not beat them.

2. Melt 40 g/1$\frac{1}{2}$ oz butter in a thick-bottomed saucepan and toss chopped ham and asparagus spears in melted butter until heated through.

3. Pour eggs into pan and cook as in basic recipe (opposite page).

4. Fold a little flaked butter into egg mixture. Spoon on to four individual heated serving plates and serve immediately. If liked, serve the egg mixture on hot toast, or in individual prebaked pastry cases heated through in a moderate (180 C, 350 F, gas 4) oven.

Serves 4

Basic Omelette

3 eggs
salt and freshly ground black pepper
generous pinch of freshly grated
 Parmesan cheese
butter

1. Break eggs into a bowl. Add 1 teaspoon water and season to taste with salt and freshly ground black pepper. Add a generous pinch of freshly grated Parmesan cheese—just enough to intensify the egg flavour without making its own taste felt—and beat vigorously until yolks and whites are well blended.

2. Melt 15 g/½ oz butter in an omelette pan over a high heat, stirring butter around so that bottom and sides of pan are entirely coated. As soon as foaming subsides and butter is on the point of changing colour, pour in eggs.

3. Now is the time to start working. As soon as eggs are in pan, take handle in your left hand and start shaking pan back and forth over heat. At the same time, scrape bottom of pan with a fork held as flat as possible in your right hand, back and forth several times in one direction, then back and forth at right angles, bringing in the sides so that eggs cook evenly. Continue working like this for a few seconds, with both hands on the move, then discard fork and allow bottom of omelette to set for a few seconds. You should feel omelette slipping freely over surface of pan, but surface of omelette should still be soft and moist.

4. Remove pan from heat. Take fork again and use it to fold nearside edge of omelette over to the centre. Then tilt pan down away from you and give the handle a few sharp knocks so that the omelette slips down the pan and the unfolded part slides up the side farthest away from you. Fold this side over the centre. Your omelette is now neatly folded in three.

5. Take a heated serving plate in your left hand and carefully tip pan up at right angles so that omelette slips out with folded edge underneath. Quickly glaze surface with a knob of butter speared on the end of a knife and serve immediately.

Serves 1

Note For a supremely light omelette, fold 1 tablespoon stiffly beaten egg white into eggs before they have set.

QUICK OMELETTE FILLINGS

Portuguese Filling

15 g/½ oz butter
2 medium-sized tomatoes, peeled,
 deseeded and chopped
salt and freshly ground black pepper

1. Melt butter in a thick-bottomed frying pan and simmer chopped tomatoes until soft. Season to taste with salt and freshly ground black pepper.

2. Cook omelette as in Steps 1, 2 and 3 of basic recipe (left) and as omelette sets, spread it with tomatoes. Fold and serve as in Steps 4 and 5 of basic recipe.

Fills 1 omelette

Florentine Filling

25 g/1 oz spinach leaves, stems removed
butter
salt and freshly ground black pepper

1. Wash spinach leaves several times in cold water, then drain. Simmer spinach in a little butter, stirring constantly, until soft. Drain and press dry.

2. Melt 25 g/1 oz butter in a thick-bottomed frying pan and heat spinach through. Season to taste with salt and freshly ground black pepper.

3. Cook omelette as in Steps 1, 2 and 3 of basic recipe (opposite page), and as omelette sets, spread it with spinach. Fold and serve as in Steps 4 and 5 of basic recipe.

Fills 1 omelette

Mushroom and Chicken Liver Filling

3 button mushrooms, sliced
2 chicken livers, chopped
15 g/½ oz butter
salt and freshly ground black pepper
1 tablespoon Quick Brown Sauce (page 50)

1. Melt butter in a thick-bottomed frying pan and sauté sliced mushrooms and chopped chicken livers until golden brown. Season generously with salt and freshly ground black pepper. Add Quick Brown Sauce.

2. Cook omelette as in Steps 1, 2 and 3 of basic recipe (opposite page), and as omelette sets, spread it with chicken livers. Fold and serve as in Steps 4 and 5 of basic recipe.

Fills 1 omelette

Individual French Omelette

3 eggs
salt and freshly ground black pepper
15 g/½ oz butter
1 tablespoon egg white, stiffly beaten
1 tablespoon freshly grated Gruyère
  cheese

1.   Break eggs into a bowl. Add 1 tablespoon water and season to taste with salt and freshly ground black pepper. Beat vigorously until yolks and whites are well blended.

2.   Melt butter in an omelette pan over a high heat, stirring butter around so that bottom and sides of pan are entirely coated. As soon as foaming subsides and butter is on the point of changing colour, pour in eggs. Cook as in basic recipe (page 62) until omelette just begins to set. Then add stiffly beaten egg white, sprinkle with freshly grated Gruyère cheese, and continue cooking until omelette sets but surface is still soft and moist.

3.   Remove pan from heat. Roll omelette on to a heated serving plate by tilting pan, starting omelette away from edge at one side and letting it roll over itself. Serve immediately.

Serves 1

Note   If desired, spread omelette with filling of your choice (page 62) before rolling.

Omelette Paysanne

butter
75 g/3 oz salt pork, diced
1 medium-sized boiled potato, diced
1 tablespoon finely chopped parsley
1 tablespoon finely chopped chives
salt and freshly ground black pepper
8 eggs

1.   Melt 25 g/1 oz butter in an omelette pan and sauté diced salt pork until golden brown. Remove from pan with a slotted spoon. Keep warm.

2.   Add diced potato to pan and sauté in remaining fats until soft and golden brown.

3.   Return salt pork to pan, add finely chopped parsley and chives, and season to taste with salt and freshly ground black pepper.

4.   Meanwhile, break eggs into a bowl. Add 1 tablespoon water and season to taste with salt and freshly ground black pepper. Beat vigorously until yolks and whites are well blended.

5.   Pour eggs into pan and cook as in Step 3 of basic recipe (page 62). Place a plate over top of pan and turn omelette out. Melt a further 15 g/½ oz butter in pan and slip omelette back into pan to brown other side. Then slip omelette on to a heated serving platter and serve immediately.

Serves 4

Omelette Basque

150 ml/¼ pint olive oil
1 green pepper, deseeded and sliced
1 red pepper, deseeded and sliced
1 Spanish onion, sliced
4 tomatoes, peeled, deseeded and
  coarsely chopped
1 clove garlic, finely chopped
1 slice Bayonne ham or cooked ham,
  diced
salt and freshly ground black pepper
8 eggs
butter

1. Heat 4 tablespoons olive oil in a thick-bottomed frying pan. Add sliced green and red peppers and onion, coarsely chopped tomatoes, finely chopped garlic and diced ham, and sauté for a few minutes. Season to taste with salt and freshly ground black pepper, and simmer for 20 minutes, or until vegetables are soft.

2. When vegetables are nearly cooked, break eggs into a bowl. Add 1 tablespoon water and season to taste with salt and freshly ground black pepper. Beat vigorously until yolks and whites are well blended.

3. Heat remaining olive oil in an omelette pan, pour in eggs and cook as in Step 3 of basic recipe (page 62).

4. Spoon vegetable mixture down centre of omelette, reserving 2 to 3 tablespoons for garnish. Slip omelette up one side of pan and fold over, in half. Then slip folded omelette out on to a heated serving platter and glaze surface with a knob of butter speared on the end of a knife. Garnish with reserved vegetable mixture and serve immediately.

Serves 4

Chinese Omelettes

25 g/1 oz butter
peanut oil
1 Spanish onion, finely chopped
6 tablespoons diced cooked roast pork
6 tablespoons chopped, peeled cooked
  prawns
50 g/2 oz fresh bean sprouts
2 teaspoons finely chopped parsley
pinch of cayenne
salt and freshly ground black pepper
soy sauce
8 eggs

1. Melt butter with 2 tablespoons peanut oil in a thick-bottomed frying pan and sauté finely chopped onion until soft but not coloured. Add diced cooked roast pork and chopped cooked prawns and continue cooking until all ingredients are golden brown.

2. Add bean sprouts and finely chopped parsley to pan and season with cayenne, salt, freshly ground black pepper and soy sauce to taste.

3. Beat eggs with a little water. Stir in meat, fish and vegetable mixture. Divide into four equal parts.

4. Heat 1 teaspoon peanut oil in an omelette pan. Pour one-quarter of the egg mixture into pan and cook as in Step 3 of basic recipe (page 62). Place a plate over top of pan and turn omelette out. Heat a further teaspoon oil in pan and slip omelette back into pan to brown other side. Slip omelette on to a heated serving platter and keep warm. Continue cooking in the same way with the remaining three parts of egg mixture. Serve immediately.

Serves 4

Fried Eggs with Sausages, Bacon and Tomatoes

4 eggs
8 pork chipolata sausages
12 rashers bacon
4 tomatoes, halved crossways
melted butter
25 g/1 oz butter
salt and freshly ground black pepper
sprigs of parsley

1. Preheat grill to high.

2. Lightly prick sausages all over with a fork and place in a grill pan. Brush with melted butter and grill under preheated grill for 6 to 8 minutes, or until browned, turning frequently to ensure even cooking. Remove from pan and keep warm.

3. Grill bacon rashers and tomato halves until cooked to your liking.

4. Meanwhile, melt 25 g/1 oz butter in a thick-bottomed frying pan. Break 1 egg at a time into a cup, season to taste with salt and freshly ground black pepper, and slide gently into pan. Fry eggs very slowly until done to your liking. Remove from pan with a spatula and drain on absorbent kitchen paper.

5. Transfer eggs, grilled sausages, bacon and tomatoes to four individual heated serving plates. Garnish with sprigs of parsley and serve immediately.

Serves 4

Baked Eggs

4 eggs
butter
double cream
salt and freshly ground black pepper
fingers of hot toast

1. Preheat oven to moderate (180 C, 350 F, gas 4).

2. Butter four individual ovenproof ramekins and spoon 1 tablespoon double cream into each dish. Break 1 egg into each dish, season to taste with salt and freshly ground black pepper, and top with a little more double cream.

3. Place dishes in a roasting tin and pour in enough hot water to come half-way up the sides of dishes. Bake in preheated oven for 12 to 15 minutes, or until whites are set. Serve immediately, with fingers of hot toast.

Serves 4

VARIATIONS

A Place lightly sautéed diced chicken livers, Italian sausage or ham in the bottom of each ramekin before adding eggs and double cream.

B Sprinkle eggs with freshly grated Parmesan cheese before topping with double cream.

C Sprinkle eggs with thin slivers or a fine dice of smoked trout, salmon or sturgeon before topping with double cream.

D Sprinkle eggs with diced Parma ham, diced sautéed mushrooms, cooked peas and freshly grated Parmesan cheese before topping with double cream.

Fried Eggs with Sausages, Bacon and Tomatoes

Baked Eggs Mornay

4 eggs
2 egg yolks
450 ml/$\frac{3}{4}$ pint hot Quick White Sauce
  (page 49)
$\frac{1}{4}$ teaspoon paprika
4 tablespoons freshly grated Gruyère
  cheese
4 tablespoons freshly grated Parmesan
  cheese
salt and freshly ground black pepper
butter

1.   Preheat oven to moderate (180 C, 350 F,
gas 4).

2.   Beat egg yolks into hot Quick White
Sauce. Add paprika, freshly grated Gruyère
cheese and half the freshly grated Parmesan
cheese, and season to taste with salt and freshly
ground black pepper.

3.   Butter a shallow casserole or four
individual ovenproof ramekins. Pour in a layer
of sauce. Break eggs into casserole, or break 1
egg into each ramekin, and sprinkle on the
remaining Parmesan cheese.

4.   Place dish or dishes in a roasting tin and
pour in enough hot water to come half-way up
the sides of the dish or dishes. Bake in
preheated oven for 12 to 15 minutes, or until
whites are set. Serve immediately.

Serves 2

Baked Eggs with Bacon and Gruyère

8 eggs
2 rashers bacon, grilled and diced
25 g/1 oz Gruyère cheese, diced
butter
salt and freshly ground black pepper
150 ml/$\frac{1}{4}$ pint double cream.

1.   Preheat oven to moderate (180 C, 350 F,
gas 4).

2.   Butter four ovenproof ramekins and
sprinkle one-quarter of the diced bacon and
cheese over the bottom of each dish. Break 2
eggs into each dish and season to taste with salt
and freshly ground black pepper. Top each
dish with 2 tablespoons double cream.

3.   Place dishes in a roasting tin and pour in
enough hot water to come half-way up the
sides of the dishes. Bake in preheated oven for
12 to 15 minutes, or until whites are set. Serve
immediately.

Serves 4

Baked Eggs with Clams

4 eggs
1 (155-g/5½-oz) can minced clams,
  drained
25 g/1 oz butter
1 tablespoon dry sherry
4 button mushrooms, diced
4–6 tablespoons double cream
salt and freshly ground black pepper
lemon juice

1. Preheat oven to moderate (180 C, 350 F, gas 4).

2. Melt butter in a thick-bottomed frying pan, add dry sherry and sauté diced mushrooms until tender.

3. Add clams and double cream to pan and continue cooking until mixture thickens slightly. Season to taste with salt, freshly ground black pepper and lemon juice.

4. Divide clam mixture between four individual ovenproof ramekins and break 1 egg into each dish.

5. Place dishes in a roasting tin and pour in enough hot water to come half-way up the sides of the dishes. Bake in preheated oven for 12 to 15 minutes, or until whites are set. Serve immediately.

Serves 4

Baked Eggs in Tomato Cases

4 eggs
4 large tomatoes
salt and freshly ground black pepper
butter

HOT MUSTARD SAUCE
25 g/1 oz butter
2 tablespoons flour
150 ml/¼ pint milk
150 ml/¼ pint single cream
1 teaspoon Dijon mustard
salt and freshly ground white pepper

1. Preheat oven to moderately hot (190 C, 375 F, gas 5).

2. Cut tops off tomatoes and scoop out seeds and pulp. Drain tomato cases.

3. Season insides of tomato cases with a little salt and freshly ground black pepper. Break 1 egg into each case, dot with butter and season to taste with salt and freshly ground black pepper. Bake in individual baking dishes, in preheated oven, for 15 to 20 minutes, or until whites are set.

4. Meanwhile, make Hot Mustard Sauce. Melt butter in a thick-bottomed saucepan. Add flour and cook for 2 to 3 minutes, stirring constantly, until flour is cooked through. Gradually add milk and single cream, stirring constantly. Add Dijon mustard and season to taste with salt and freshly ground white pepper. Cover and simmer for 5 minutes, or until smooth and well blended.

5. Top baked eggs with Hot Mustard Sauce and serve immediately.

Serves 4

Vegetable Appetiser Salad with Anchovy Dressing

olive oil
red wine vinegar
salt and freshly ground black pepper
100 g/4 oz bean sprouts, trimmed
8 tomatoes, quartered
1 small cucumber, thinly sliced
2 small green peppers, deseeded and cut
  into thin strips
100 g/4 oz button mushrooms, thinly
  sliced
lettuce leaves
2 hard-boiled eggs, halved

ANCHOVY DRESSING
150 ml/¼ pint olive oil
4 anchovy fillets, finely chopped
juice of 1 lemon
1 teaspoon capers
freshly ground black pepper

1. Combine a little olive oil and red wine vinegar in five separate bowls and season each to taste with salt and freshly ground black pepper.

2. Add bean sprouts to the first bowl, quartered tomatoes to the second, thinly sliced cucumber to the third, green pepper strips to the fourth and thinly sliced mushrooms to the fifth. Toss all ingredients in their bowls. Drain.

3. To make Anchovy Dressing, warm olive oil and combine with finely chopped anchovy fillets, mashing together until smooth and well blended. Add lemon juice and capers and season to taste with freshly ground black pepper.

4. Arrange lettuce leaves on a serving platter and assemble salad on leaves. Garnish with halved hard-boiled eggs, pour over Anchovy Dressing and serve.

Serves 4 to 6

Curried Hard-Boiled Eggs

2 hard-boiled eggs, cut into 8–12 even-
  sized slices
4–6 slices white bread
butter
paprika

CURRIED MAYONNAISE
4 tablespoons mayonnaise
2 teaspoons curry paste
pinch of ground turmeric

1. Preheat grill to high.

2. To make Curried Mayonnaise, combine mayonnaise and curry paste and add the ground turmeric for colour.

3. Toast bread slices under preheated grill and cut into 8 to 12 even-sized rounds.

4. Butter toast rounds, top with a slice of hard-boiled egg and mask with Curried Mayonnaise. Sprinkle each round with paprika and serve.

Serves 4

Vegetable Appetiser Salad with Anchovy Dressing

Creamed Eggs

6 hard-boiled eggs (see below, Step 1)
50 g/2 oz butter
2 tablespoons flour
300 ml/½ pint hot milk
salt and freshly ground black pepper
freshly grated nutmeg, or cayenne
4 slices hot buttered toast
2 tablespoons finely chopped parsley or
  chives

1.   Cool hard-boiled eggs by plunging them into cold water as soon as they are cooked. Carefully remove shells and cut eggs into quarters.

2.   Melt butter in a thick-bottomed saucepan, add flour and cook for 2 to 3 minutes, stirring constantly, until flour is cooked through. Gradually add hot milk and cook, stirring vigorously, until sauce is thick and smooth. Season generously with salt and freshly ground black pepper, and add freshly grated nutmeg, or cayenne, to taste.

3.   Add quartered hard-boiled eggs to sauce and heat through. Spoon creamed eggs on to hot buttered toast, sprinkle with finely chopped parsley or chives, and serve immediately.

Serves 4

Creamed Eggs à la King

1 x recipe quantity Creamed Eggs (left)
50 g/2 oz button mushrooms, thinly sliced
50 g/2 oz frozen peas
1 canned pimiento, cut into thin strips
4 slices hot buttered toast
2 tablespoons finely chopped parsley or
  chives

1.   Add thinly sliced mushrooms, frozen peas and pimiento strips to Creamed Eggs and heat through.

2.   Spoon egg mixture on to hot buttered toast. Sprinkle with finely chopped parsley or chives, and serve immediately.

Serves 4

Egg Croquettes

8 hard-boiled eggs, chopped
50 g/2 oz butter
4 tablespoons finely chopped onion
4 tablespoons flour
150 ml/¼ pint hot milk
4 tablespoons finely chopped parsley
¼ teaspoon paprika
pinch of cayenne
salt and freshly ground black pepper
2 eggs
fresh breadcrumbs
oil for deep drying
1 x recipe quantity French Tomato Sauce
  (page 54)

1.   Melt butter in a thick-bottomed saucepan, and sauté finely chopped onion until soft but not coloured. Add flour and cook, stirring constantly, until flour is cooked through.

Gradually add hot milk and cook, stirring vigorously, until sauce is thick and smooth.

2. Add chopped hard-boiled eggs and finely chopped parsley to pan and season with paprika, cayenne, and salt and freshly ground black pepper to taste. Spread evenly in a roasting tin. Chill briefly in a freezer.

3. Meanwhile, lightly beat eggs with 2 tablespoons water and pour into a shallow dish. Place breadcrumbs in another dish.

4. Cut egg mixture into 16 small rectangles and shape into croquettes. Dip each croquette in beaten egg, draining carefully. Then roll in breadcrumbs, patting coating on firmly.

5. Heat oil in a deep saucepan or deep-fryer to a temperature of 190 C, 375 F; a 2.5-cm/1-in cube of day-old bread takes 1 minute to turn crisp and golden brown at this temperature.

6. Deep fry croquettes in preheated oil for 1 minute, or until golden brown. Drain on absorbent kitchen paper. Serve immediately, with French Tomato Sauce (page 54).

Serves 4

Oeufs Moulés

butter
salt and freshly ground black pepper
4 eggs
fingers of hot toast

1. Preheat oven to moderate (180 C, 350 F, gas 4).

2. Generously butter four individual dariole moulds and season to taste with salt and freshly ground black pepper. Break 1 egg into each mould.

3. Place moulds in a roasting tin and pour in enough hot water to come half-way up the sides of the moulds. Bake in preheated oven for 12 to 15 minutes, or until whites are set.

4. Turn moulds out on to four individual heated serving plates and serve immediately, with fingers of hot toast.

Serves 4

VARIATIONS

A Before adding eggs, sprinkle insides of dariole moulds with finely chopped parsley or chives, or with finely chopped mushrooms which you have sautéed in butter until golden brown.

B Turn moulds out into individual prebaked pastry cases and pour over one of the following sauces:
(i) a purée of peeled, deseeded and chopped tomatoes, softened in butter with a hint of finely chopped shallot, dried thyme, salt and freshly ground black pepper;
(ii) a purée of poached artichoke hearts enriched with Chicken Velouté Sauce (page 53) and double cream;
(iii) a purée of poached asparagus tips enriched with Chicken Velouté Sauce (page 53) and double cream.

C Turn moulds out on to a base of poached artichoke hearts, baked mushroom caps or tomato cases. Mask eggs with Béchamel Sauce (page 52), or Hollandaise Sauce (page 55).

CHAPTER SIX

FISH AND SHELLFISH

Medallions of Salmon with Cucumber Sauce

4 thin (100 to 150-g/4 to 5-oz) salmon
  steaks, shaped into ovals
melted butter
olive oil
12 blanched mange-tout peas, sliced
4 carrot 'flowers' or tomato 'roses'

DRY MARINADE
½ chicken stock cube, crumbled
4 tablespoons lemon juice
cayenne

CUCUMBER SAUCE
½ medium-sized cucumber, peeled and
  grated
1 tablespoon chopped parsley
3 tablespoons double cream
¼ teaspoon salt

1.   Combine dry marinade ingredients in a porcelain or earthenware (not metal) bowl.

2.   Toss salmon medallions in marinade and allow to stand for 15 minutes.

3.   Meanwhile, make Cucumber Sauce. Combine grated cucumber and chopped parsley. Combine double cream and salt and whip until soft peaks form. Fold into cucumber. Pass through a fine sieve into a serving bowl, pressing cucumber against sieve to extract utmost in flavour.

4.   Brush medallions with melted butter.

5.   Brush a thick-bottomed frying pan with olive oil and sauté salmon medallions for 4 minutes. Turn medallions over, brush with melted butter and continue to sauté for a further 3 to 4 minutes, or until fish flakes easily with a fork. Transfer 1 medallion to each of four heated serving dishes and surround by Cucumber Sauce. Garnish each plate with 3 sliced mange-tout peas and a carrot 'flower' or tomato 'rose' and serve immediately.

Serves 4

Medallions of Salmon with Cucumber Sauce

Barbecued Red Mullet

8–12 red mullet, cleaned and scaled
olive oil
salt and freshly ground black pepper
lemon juice
dried fennel stalks, or fresh or dried
  sprigs of rosemary
2 tablespoons coarsely chopped parsley
lemon quarters

FINES HERBES BUTTER
4–6 tablespoons melted butter
1 tablespoon chopped parsley
1 teaspoon chopped tarragon
1 teaspoon chopped chives
juice of $\frac{1}{2}$ lemon
salt and freshly ground black pepper

1. To make Fines Herbes Butter, combine first five ingredients and season to taste with salt and freshly ground black pepper.

2. Brush prepared red mullet with olive oil and season generously, inside and out, with salt, freshly ground black pepper and lemon juice.

3. Place mullet on rack of a charcoal grill, with a few dried fennel stalks, or fresh or dried sprigs of rosemary, underneath. Grill over hot charcoal for 5 to 8 minutes on each side, basting from time to time with a little more olive oil.

4. Transfer mullet to a heated serving platter. Sprinkle with coarsely chopped parsley and serve immediately, with lemon quarters and Fines Herbes Butter.

Serves 4 to 6

Greek Skewered Cod with Skordalia Sauce

675 g/1$\frac{1}{2}$ lb thick end of cod fillet, skinned
  and cut into 40 even-sized cubes
4 tablespoons olive oil
2 tablespoons lemon juice
bay leaf, crumbled
salt and freshly ground black pepper
50 g/2 oz butter
16 button onions
4 firm tomatoes, quartered
shredded lettuce

SKORDALIA SAUCE
2 cloves garlic, chopped
3 tablespoons finely chopped parsley
1 large boiled potato, or an equal
  quantity of moist fresh breadcrumbs
50 g/2 oz blanched almonds, crushed
4 tablespoons red wine vinegar
150 ml/$\frac{1}{4}$ pint olive oil
salt and freshly ground black pepper

1. To make Skordalia Sauce, combine chopped garlic, finely chopped parsley, boiled potato or moist breadcrumbs, and crushed almonds in a mortar and pound to a smooth paste. Add red wine vinegar and olive oil, little by little, pounding until the mixture acquires the consistency of a thick mayonnaise. Season to taste with salt and freshly ground black pepper.

2. Combine olive oil, lemon juice and crumbled bay leaf and season to taste with salt and freshly ground black pepper. Toss cod cubes in marinade and allow to stand for a few minutes. Drain. Reserve marinade.

3. Meanwhile, melt 15 g/½ oz butter in a thick-bottomed frying pan and sauté button onions until soft but not coloured.

4. Thread each of eight metal skewers with 5 fish cubes, 2 tomato quarters and 2 button onions. Start and finish each skewer with 2 fish cubes, and arrange the tomato quarters, button onions and remaining fish cube between.

5. Melt remaining butter in another frying pan and sauté skewers for 1½ to 2 minutes on each side, or until the fish flakes easily with a fork, basting frequently with reserved marinade. Serve on a bed of shredded lettuce, accompanied by Skordalia Sauce.

Serves 4

Truite Meunière

1 (350 to 400-g/12 to 14-oz) rainbow trout, cleaned
salt
flour
25 g/1 oz butter
2 teaspoons olive oil
juice of ½ lemon
2 teaspoons finely chopped parsley
lemon slices
sprigs of watercress

1. Sprinkle prepared rainbow trout with salt and toss it in flour, shaking off excess.

2. Melt 15 g/½ oz butter with the olive oil in a thick-bottomed frying pan and sauté trout for 5 minutes on each side, or until delicately brown. Transfer from pan with a fish slice to a heated serving platter. Keep warm.

3. Pour off excess fats from pan. Melt remaining butter in pan with lemon juice and allow to brown slightly.

4. Pour butter sauce over trout and sprinkle with finely chopped parsley. Garnish with lemon slices and sprigs of watercress and serve immediately.

Serves 1

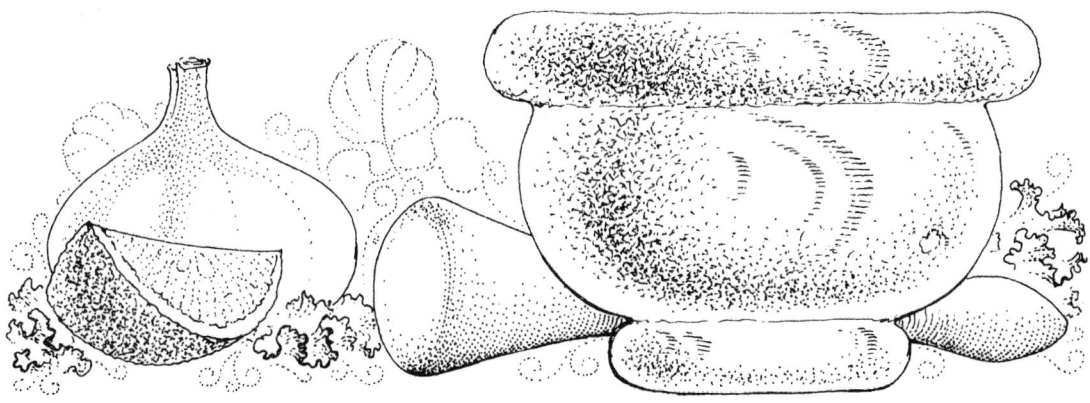

Sole Michel Oliver

12 (50-g/2-oz) sole fillets
3 medium-sized carrots, cut into thin
  strips 5 cm/2 in long
2 leeks, white parts only, cut into thin
  strips 5 cm/2 in long
1 large turnip, cut into thin strips
  5 cm/2 in long
1 stick celery, cut into thin strips
  5 cm/2 in long
salt
butter
freshly ground black pepper
½ chicken stock cube, crumbled
1 teaspoon cornflour, mixed with 6
  tablespoons dry white wine
150 ml/¼ pint double cream

1. Cook carrot, leek, turnip and celery strips
in boiling salted water for 3 to 5 minutes, or
until just tender. Drain and refresh under cold
running water. Drain again.

2. Lightly score each sole fillet three times
lengthways. Roll up, with the shiny side on the
inside of the roll. Place rolls side by side, with
folded edge down, in a buttered frying pan.
Season to taste with salt and freshly ground
black pepper.

3. Combine crumbled ½ chicken stock cube,
cornflour mixture and double cream in a thick-
bottomed saucepan. Bring to the boil, stirring
constantly.

4. Pour sauce over sole rolls and cook over a
high heat until sauce begins to bubble again.
Cover and continue to cook for 4 minutes, or
until fish flakes easily with a fork. Remove rolls
from pan with a slotted spoon. Keep warm.

Sole Michel Oliver

5. Bring sauce to the boil again. Add
vegetables and cook over a high heat until
sauce is reduced to half the original quantity.

6. Transfer 3 sole rolls to each of four
individual serving dishes. Garnish with
vegetables, spoon over sauce and serve
immediately.

Serves 4

Sole Meunière

1 (350 to 400-g/12 to 14-oz) sole, skinned
salt
flour
15 g/½ oz butter
2 teaspoons olive oil
few drops of lemon juice
2 teaspoons finely chopped parsley

1. Sprinkle prepared sole with salt and toss it
in flour, shaking off excess.

2. Melt 15 g/½ oz butter with the olive oil in a
thick-bottomed frying pan. Sauté the sole for 5
to 6 minutes on each side, or until delicately
brown.

3. Transfer sole to a heated serving platter
and pour over pan juices. Squeeze over lemon
juice, sprinkle with finely chopped parsley and
serve immediately.

Serves 1

VARIATION

A Cook as in Step 2 of basic recipe (above).
Transfer to a heated serving platter and keep
warm. Melt 25 g/1 oz butter in another pan and
sauté 8 halved, seedless white grapes for 4 to 5
minutes, or until golden brown. Pour grapes,
together with pan juices, over sole.

Fish Fillets Meunière

12 (50-g/2-oz) sole fillets
salt and freshly ground black pepper
flour
175 g/6 oz butter
4 tablespoons lemon juice
4 teaspoons chopped parsley
lemon quarters
grilled tomatoes

1.   Season sole fillets to taste with salt and freshly ground black pepper, and toss them in flour, shaking off excess.

2.   Melt 100 g/4 oz butter in a thick-bottomed frying pan and sauté fillets for 2 to 3 minutes on each side, or until delicately brown. Transfer from pan with a fish slice to a heated serving platter. Keep warm.

3.   Pour off excess fat from pan. Melt remaining butter in pan with lemon juice and allow to brown slightly.

4.   Pour butter sauce over fillets and sprinkle with chopped parsley. Garnish with lemon quarters and grilled tomatoes and serve immediately.

Serves 4

Fish Fillets in Foil

4 (50-g/2-oz) sole fillets
75 g/3 oz butter
2 tablespoons finely chopped onion
225 g/8 oz button mushrooms, finely
  chopped
2 tablespoons finely chopped parsley
2 tablespoons flour
150 ml/$\frac{1}{4}$ pint milk
6 tablespoons double cream
salt and freshly ground black pepper

1.   Preheat oven to moderately hot (200 C, 400 F, gas 6).

2.   Melt 25 g/1 oz butter in a thick-bottomed saucepan and sauté finely chopped onion until soft but not coloured.

3.   Add finely chopped mushrooms and parsley to pan and cook until mushrooms are tender. Add flour and cook for 2 to 3 minutes, stirring constantly, until flour is cooked through. Gradually add milk and double cream and cook, stirring vigorously, until thick and smooth. Season to taste with salt and freshly ground black pepper. Keep warm.

4.   Melt remaining butter in a thick-bottomed frying pan and sauté fish fillets for 2 to 3 minutes on each side, or until delicately brown.

5.   Meanwhile, cut four large hearts, about 23 cm/9 in long and 30 cm/11 in wide, out of aluminium foil.

6.   Spread one half of each heart with a little mushroom sauce. Lay 1 fish fillet on top of sauce and top with remaining sauce. Fold foil over and seal edges by crimping together. Place on a baking sheet and bake in preheated oven for 10 minutes. Transfer to a heated serving platter. Slit edges of foil, roll back and serve immediately.

Serves 2

Cod Provençale

4 (150-g/5-oz) cod steaks
salt and freshly ground black pepper
butter
3 tablespoons finely chopped onion
2 tablespoons finely chopped parsley
1 teaspoon mashed garlic
pinch of dried thyme
2 large ripe tomatoes, peeled, deseeded
 and chopped
100 g/4 oz button mushrooms, thinly
sliced and sautéed in butter
250 ml/8 fl oz dry white wine

1. Season cod steaks to taste with salt and freshly ground black pepper.

2. Place steaks in a buttered flameproof gratin dish large enough to take fish in one layer, and sprinkle with finely chopped onion and parsley, mashed garlic and dried thyme. Add peeled, deseeded and chopped tomatoes, thinly sliced and sautéed mushrooms, and dry white wine. Cover with buttered greaseproof paper and simmer for 15 to 20 minutes, or until the fish flakes easily with a fork. Transfer fish from pan to a heated serving platter. Keep warm.

3. Cook pan juices over a high heat until reduced to half the original quantity. Stir in 15 g/½ oz butter.

4. Pour sauce over steaks and serve immediately.

Serves 4

Italian Poached Cod

4 (150-g/5-oz) cod steaks
salt
juice of 1 lemon
freshly ground black pepper

SAUCE
4 tablespoons finely chopped onion
4 tablespoons finely chopped parsley
2 cloves garlic, finely chopped
150 ml/¼ pint olive oil
juice of ½ lemon
salt and freshly ground black pepper

1. Place cod steaks in a thick-bottomed frying pan large enough to take steaks in one layer. Cover with salted water and season with lemon juice, and freshly ground black pepper to taste. Bring to the boil. Turn off heat, cover and allow to steep in hot water for 10 to 12 minutes, or until the fish flakes easily with a fork. Drain on absorbent kitchen paper. Transfer to a serving dish. Allow to cool, then chill until needed.

2. Meanwhile, combine all the sauce ingredients and chill.

3. When ready to serve, pour the sauce over the cod steaks.

Serves 4

Chinese Steamed Fish with Ginger and Lime

2 (350-g/12-oz) whiting or rainbow trout,
  cleaned
4–6 slices fresh root ginger
2 tablespoons lime juice
4–6 dried mushrooms
12 French beans, sliced diagonally into
  thin strips
1 clove garlic, finely chopped
4 spring onions, green parts only, cut
  into 5-mm/$\frac{1}{4}$-in dice
4 tablespoons peanut oil
2 tablespoons soy sauce
1 tablespoon cornflour, mixed with 2
  tablespoons water
1 teaspoon sesame oil
freshly ground black pepper
strips of lemon peel, tied into knots

1.   Place prepared whiting or rainbow trout in
a shallow dish.

2.   Soak dried mushrooms in a little hot water
until soft. Cut into thin strips, squeeze dry and
add to dish.

3.   Add ginger slices and French bean strips to
dish.

4.   Combine lime juice, finely chopped garlic,
diced spring onion, peanut oil, soy sauce,
cornflour mixture and sesame oil, and season to
taste with freshly ground black pepper. Pour
over fish.

5.   Place dish in a large steamer, or on a rack
set in a thick-bottomed saucepan, containing
5 cm/2 in of rapidly boiling water. Cover and
steam for 15 minutes, or until fish flakes easily
with a fork. Transfer to a heated serving
platter. Spoon over mushrooms, ginger,

French beans and sauce, garnish with lemon
knots and serve immediately.

Serves 2

Lime-Steamed Sea Bass in the Packet

4 (175 to 225-g/6 to 8-oz) sea bass fillets
4 thin slices lime
75 g/3 oz butter
4 tablespoons lime juice
6 spring onions, diced
1 tablespoon finely slivered fresh root
  ginger
1 teaspoon finely slivered garlic
salt and freshly ground black pepper

1.   Preheat oven to moderate (180 C, 350 F,
gas 4).

2.   Cut four rectangles of foil large enough to
envelop sea bass fillets completely. Place 1 fillet
on each rectangle and top with a lime slice.

3.   Melt butter in a thick-bottomed frying
pan. Add lime juice, diced spring onion and
finely slivered fresh root ginger and garlic.
Season to taste with salt and freshly ground
black pepper, and cook until sauce just begins
to bubble.

4.   Spoon sauce over fillets, fold foil over and
seal edges by crimping together. Place on a
baking sheet and 'steam' in preheated oven for
20 minutes. Transfer to a heated serving dish.
Slit edges of foil, roll back and serve
immediately.

Serves 4

Chinese Steamed Fish with Ginger and Lime

Oven-Fried Plaice à la Niçoise

4 (150-g/5-oz) plaice fillets
150 ml/¼ pint milk
100 g/4 oz fresh breadcrumbs
4 tablespoons finely chopped parsley
2 cloves garlic, finely chopped
grated rind of ½ lemon
½ teaspoon dried thyme
salt and freshly ground black pepper
50 g/2 oz butter
2 tablespoons olive oil
paprika
1 lemon, cut into 8 wedges

1.   Preheat oven to hot (220 C, 425 F, gas 7).

2.   Pour milk into a shallow dish. In another dish, combine breadcrumbs, finely chopped parsley and garlic, grated lemon rind and dried thyme, and season to taste with salt and freshly ground black pepper.

3.   Dip plaice fillets in milk, draining carefully, and roll them in breadcrumb mixture, patting coating on firmly.

4.   Place butter and olive oil in an ovenproof gratin dish large enough to take fillets in one layer, and place dish in preheated oven. When butter has melted and is sizzling, place fillets in dish. Return to oven and cook for 10 to 12 minutes, or until the fish flakes easily with a fork, turning once. Transfer to a heated serving dish, dust with paprika and serve immediately, garnished with lemon wedges.

Serves 2

Oven-Fried Fish Fillets

12 (75-g/3-oz) plaice fillets
salt and freshly ground black pepper
paprika
250 ml/8 fl oz milk
100 g/4 oz fresh breadcrumbs
butter
4 tablespoons melted butter
lemon wedges

1.   Preheat oven to very hot (240 C, 475 F, gas 9).

2.   Season plaice fillets to taste with salt, freshly ground black pepper and paprika.

3.   Pour milk into a shallow dish. Place breadcrumbs in another dish.

4.   Dip fillets in milk, draining carefully, and roll them in breadcrumbs, patting coating on firmly. Place in a buttered, ovenproof gratin dish. Pour over melted butter and cook in preheated oven for 10 to 12 minutes, or until the fish flakes easily with a fork. Transfer to a heated serving platter, garnish with lemon wedges and serve immediately.

Serves 6

Deep-Fried Fish

1 kg/2 lb sole fillets, cut into 1-cm/½-in
  strips
salt and freshly ground black pepper
1 egg
1 tablespoon milk
100 g/4 oz fresh breadcrumbs
oil for deep frying
1 x recipe quantity Tartare Sauce (page
  56)

1. Season sole strips to taste with salt and
freshly ground black pepper.

2. Lightly beat egg with milk and pour into a
shallow dish. Place breadcrumbs in another
dish.

3. Dip sole strips in beaten egg mixture,
draining carefully, and roll them in
breadcrumbs, patting coating on firmly.

4. Heat oil in a deep saucepan or deep-fryer to
a temperature of 190 C, 375 F; a 2.5-cm/1-in
cube of day-old bread takes 1 minute to turn
crisp and golden brown at this temperature.

5. Deep-fry sole strips in preheated oil for 3
to 5 minutes, or until golden brown. Drain on
absorbent kitchen paper. Transfer to a heated
serving dish and serve immediately, accompanied by Tartare Sauce.

Serves 6

Creamed Salmon and Corn

1 (213-g/7½-oz) can salmon, drained and
  flaked
1 (198-g/7-oz) can sweet corn, drained
25 g/1 oz butter
4 tablespoons flour
1 teaspoon sugar
salt and freshly ground black pepper
450 ml/¾ pint milk
1 tablespoon chopped canned pimiento
2 teaspoons finely chopped parsley
hot toast

1. Melt butter in a thick-bottomed saucepan.
Add flour and sugar, season to taste with salt
and freshly ground black pepper, and cook for
2 to 3 minutes, stirring constantly, until flour is
cooked through. Gradually add milk and cook,
stirring vigorously, until thick and smooth.

2. Add flaked salmon, sweet corn and
chopped pimiento to pan and heat through.
Transfer to four individual preheated
ramekins. Sprinkle with finely chopped parsley
and serve immediately, with hot toast.

Serves 4

Deep-Fried Mussel and Bacon Brochettes

48 cooked mussels, removed from shells
225 g/8 oz lean bacon, in one piece
2 eggs, beaten
salt and freshly ground black pepper
fresh breadcrumbs
oil for deep frying
1 × recipe quantity Béarnaise Sauce (page 55)

1.   Cut bacon into 36 pieces, to the size of mussels.

2.   Pour beaten eggs into a shallow dish and season generously with salt and freshly ground black pepper. Place breadcrumbs in another dish.

3.   Dip mussels and bacon pieces in seasoned egg, draining carefully, and roll in breadcrumbs, patting coating on firmly. Thread mussels and bacon pieces alternately on to 12 skewers, starting and finishing with mussels.

4.   Heat oil in a deep saucepan or deep-fryer to a temperature of 190 C, 375 F; a 2.5-cm/1-in cube of day-old bread takes 1 minute to turn crisp and golden brown at this temperature.

5.   Deep-fry brochettes in preheated oil for 4 to 5 minutes, or until golden brown. Drain on absorbent kitchen paper. Transfer to a heated serving dish and serve immediately, accompanied by Béarnaise Sauce.

Serves 4

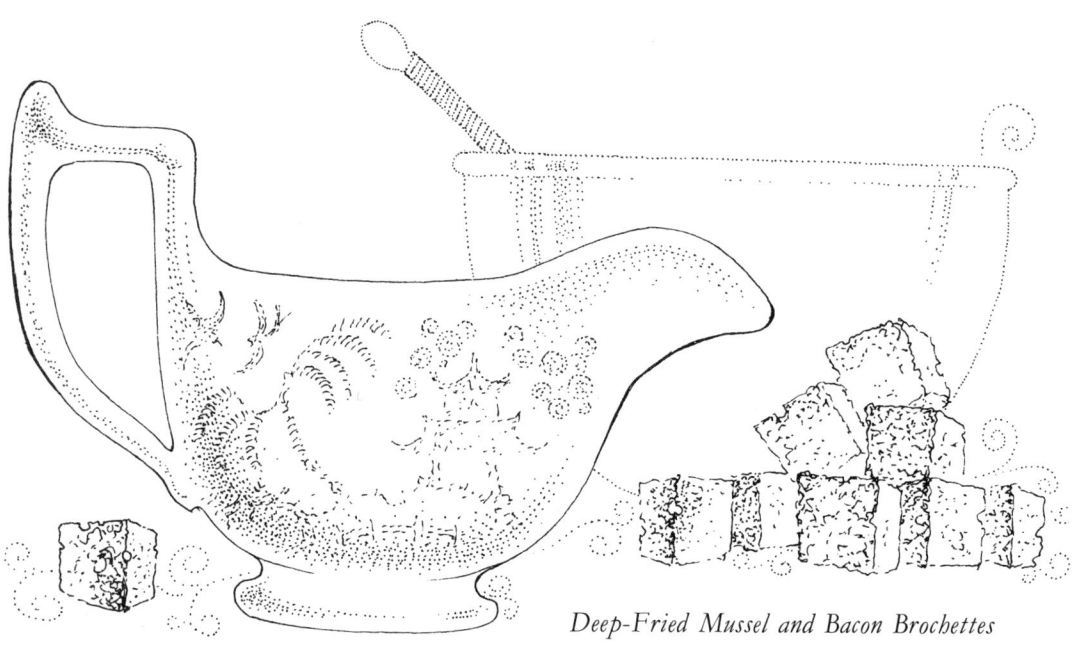

Deep-Fried Mussel and Bacon Brochettes

Curried Shrimps

450 g/1 lb cooked shrimps, peeled
25 g/1 oz butter
1 Spanish onion, chopped
1 small green pepper, deseeded and
  chopped
1 stick celery, chopped
2 tablespoons flour
1–2 tablespoons curry paste
3 teaspoons soy sauce
1 (396-g/14-oz) can peeled Italian
  tomatoes, drained
225 g/8 oz boiled rice

1. Melt butter in a thick-bottomed frying pan and sauté chopped onion, green pepper and celery until onion is soft but not coloured.

2. Add flour, curry paste, soy sauce, tomatoes and 250 ml/8 fl oz water to pan. Cover and simmer for 20 minutes, or until thick and smooth.

3. Add cooked shrimps to sauce and heat through. Serve immediately, on a bed of boiled rice.

Serves 4

Curried Shrimps with Courgettes

1 (198-g/7-oz) can shrimps, drained and
  chopped
12 medium-sized courgettes
salt
25 g/1 oz butter
1 tablespoon olive oil
1 tablespoon finely chopped onion
1 medium-sized red pepper, deseeded
  and finely chopped
1 teaspoon curry powder
**pinch each of ground turmeric and
  cayenne**
2 tablespoons flour
4 tablespoons single cream
50 g/2 oz fresh breadcrumbs

1. Preheat oven to moderate (180 C, 350 F, gas 4).

2. Cut courgettes in half lengthways and blanch in boiling salted water for 5 minutes. Drain. Hollow out centres, being careful not to break skins, and chop flesh finely.

3. Melt butter with olive oil in a thick-bottomed frying pan. Add finely chopped onion and red pepper, curry powder, $\frac{1}{2}$ teaspoon salt, turmeric, cayenne, flour and single cream. Cook, stirring constantly, until thick and smooth.

4. Add chopped shrimps and courgette flesh to pan and heat through. Correct seasoning.

5. Fill courgette shells with curried shrimp mixture, sprinkle with breadcrumbs and cook in preheated oven for 15 minutes, or until golden brown. Transfer to a heated serving platter and serve immediately.

Serves 6

Quick Lobster Newburg

4 (675 g to 1-kg/1½ to 2-lb) cooked
  lobsters
50 g/2 oz butter
4 tablespoons cognac, warmed
2 egg yolks, beaten
300 ml/½ pint double cream
salt and freshly ground black pepper
cayenne
paprika
350 g/12 oz boiled rice

1. Remove the two claws from each lobster and crack them. Split each lobster in half lengthways. Remove lobster meat from shells and claws and cut into large cubes.

2. Melt butter in a thick-bottomed frying pan and sauté lobster cubes until heated through. Pour over warmed cognac and flame. Reserve.

3. Combine beaten egg yolks and double cream in the top of a double saucepan. Cook over hot but not boiling water, stirring constantly, until sauce coats the back of a spoon.

4. Add lobster cubes and cooking juices to sauce and heat through; be careful not to let sauce curdle. Season to taste with salt, freshly ground black pepper, cayenne and paprika, and serve immediately, on a bed of boiled rice.

Serves 4

Shrimp Tempura

1 kg/2 lb cooked shrimps, peeled, tail left
  unpeeled
oil for deep frying

TEMPURA SAUCE
4 tablespoons dry sherry
1 tablespoon soy sauce
2 teaspoons sugar
pinch of ground ginger

BATTER
100 g/4 oz flour, sifted
½ teaspoon salt
2 eggs, beaten

1. To make Tempura Sauce, combine dry sherry, soy sauce, sugar and ground ginger. Pour into four to six individual bowls—one for each guest.

2. To make the batter, combine sifted flour and salt. Add beaten eggs and 225 ml/7½ fl oz water and beat until just blended.

3. Heat oil in a deep saucepan or deep-fryer to a temperature of 190 C, 375 F; a 2.5-cm/1-in cube of day-old bread takes 1 minute to turn crisp and golden brown at this temperature.

4. Dip shrimps in batter and deep-fry in preheated oil for 2 to 3 minutes, or until golden brown. Drain on absorbent kitchen paper. Transfer to four to six individual heated serving plates and serve immediately, accompanied by individual bowls of Tempura Sauce.

Serves 4 to 6

CHAPTER SEVEN

FROM THE GRILL

Basic Grilled Hamburger

1 kg/2 lb lean sirloin or rump steak,
  minced
4 tablespoons finely chopped onion
salt and freshly ground black pepper
melted butter
olive oil
8 buns, split and toasted

1.   Preheat grill to high.

2.   Combine minced sirloin or rump steak and finely chopped onion, and season to taste with salt and freshly ground black pepper. Form into eight flat rounds, 2 cm/$\frac{3}{4}$ in thick. Brush with melted butter.

3.   Brush rack of grill pan with olive oil and place hamburgers on rack. Grill under preheated grill, 7.5 cm/3 in from heat, for 1$\frac{1}{2}$ minutes on each side for rare hamburgers, 3 minutes on each side for medium, and 4 minutes on each side for well done. Serve immediately, in toasted buns.

Serves 8

VARIATIONS

A   Combine 100 g/4 oz minced sirloin or rump steak, 1 teaspoon each finely chopped parsley and onion, and season to taste with salt and freshly ground black pepper. Form into one flat round 2 cm/$\frac{3}{4}$ in thick and cook as in basic recipe (left).

B   Combine 100 g/4 oz minced sirloin or rump steak, 1 teaspoon tomato ketchup and $\frac{1}{4}$ teaspoon Worcestershire sauce, and season to taste with salt and freshly ground black pepper. Form into one flat round 2 cm/$\frac{3}{4}$ in thick and cook as in basic recipe (left).

C   Combine 100 g/4 oz minced sirloin or rump steak and $\frac{1}{4}$ teaspoon soy sauce. Season with 2 drops of Tabasco sauce, and salt and freshly ground black pepper to taste. Form into one flat round 2 cm/$\frac{3}{4}$ in thick and cook as in basic recipe (left).

Hamburger fillings and garnishes can be varied tremendously to suit individual taste

Grilled Minute Steak

1 (175 to 225-g/6 to 8-oz) sirloin steak,
trimmed
freshly ground black pepper
melted butter
1 teaspoon each chopped chives and
parsley

1.   Preheat grill to high.

2.   Place sirloin steak between two sheets of
wet cling film. Beat steak with a meat bat until
it has almost trebled in length and width and is
not less than 3 mm/$\frac{1}{8}$ in thick. Season generously with freshly ground black pepper and
brush with melted butter.

3.   Line grill pan with aluminium foil. Place
steak on foil and grill under preheated grill for
1 minute on each side. Transfer to a heated
serving plate and pour over pan juices.
Sprinkle with chopped chives and parsley and
serve immediately.

Serves 1

VARIATIONS

A   Grill minute steak as in basic recipe
(above), but serve with Pizzaiola Sauce.

To make Pizzaiola Sauce for four servings, heat
2 tablespoons olive oil and sauté 1 sliced garlic
clove until soft but not coloured. Add 1 (227-
g/8-oz) can peeled Italian tomatoes, drained
and chopped. Season to taste with salt and
freshly ground black pepper and cook over a
high heat for 15 minutes, stirring occasionally.
Add 1 tablespoon finely chopped parsley and $\frac{1}{4}$
teaspoon dried oregano before serving.

B   Grill minute steak as in basic recipe
(above), but serve with a round of Roquefort
Butter.

To make Roquefort Butter for four servings,
cream together 25 g/1 oz Roquefort cheese,
50 g/2 oz butter, juice of $\frac{1}{2}$ lemon and 2
tablespoons finely chopped mixed parsley,
chervil and chives. Season to taste with freshly
ground black pepper. Chill until firm.

Charcoal-Grilled Steak

1 (175 to 225-g/6 to 8-oz) sirloin or rump
 steak, 5 cm/2 in thick, trimmed
freshly ground black pepper
melted butter
olive oil

1.   Season sirloin or rump steak generously
with freshly ground black pepper and brush
with melted butter.

2.   Brush rack of charcoal grill with olive oil,
place steak on rack and sear on both sides. Set
rack 10 cm/4 in from hot charcoal and grill for
10 minutes on each side for a rare steak, 20
minutes on each side for medium, and 25
minutes on each side for well done. Slice in thin
diagonal slices across the grain just before
serving.

Serves 1

VARIATIONS

London Broil

Generously season a 175 to 225-g/6 to 8-oz
flank steak with freshly ground black pepper,
and a dash of Tabasco sauce if desired. Grill
over hot charcoal, 10 cm/4 in from heat, for 2
minutes on each side. This steak should be
served very very rare or it will be tough. Slice
in thin diagonal slices across the grain before
serving.

Lamb Steak

Ask your butcher for young tender lamb from a small animal. Combine 1 tablespoon olive oil, 1 teaspoon lemon juice and ½ finely chopped garlic clove. Flavour a 2.5-cm/1-in lamb steak with the dressing and grill over hot charcoal, 10 cm/4 in from heat, for 5 minutes on each side for a pink steak and 7 minutes on each side for a well-done steak.

Gammon Steak

Cut rind off a 1-cm/½-in thick gammon steak and snip round edges at intervals to prevent curling during grilling. Season steak generously with freshly ground black pepper and brush with melted butter. Grill over hot charcoal, 10 cm/4 in from heat, for 6 minutes on each side.

Chops

One of the best outdoor grills I have ever tasted was also the simplest: thick veal chops cooked with halved tomatoes and large mushroom caps. Before being grilled over hot charcoal the chops and vegetables were seasoned generously with dried rosemary, salt and freshly ground black pepper, and were brushed with melted butter. The fat from the chop and the flames gave a wonderful flavour.

Lamb chops, veal chops and pork chops can all be grilled to perfection over hot charcoal. Grill a 2.5-cm/1-in thick lamb chop over hot charcoal, 10 cm/4 in from heat, for 5 minutes on each side for a pink chop and 7 minutes on each side for a well-done chop; grill a 2.5-cm/1-in thick veal chop for 4 minutes on each side for a pink chop and 6 minutes for a well-done chop; and grill a 2.5-cm/1-in thick pork chop for 7 minutes on each side.

Grilled Sirloin Steaks with Mustard Glaze

4 (175 to 225-g/6 to 8-oz) sirloin steaks, each 2.5 cm/1 in thick, trimmed
3 tablespoons Dijon mustard
3 tablespoons soft brown sugar
freshly ground black pepper
olive oil

1. Preheat grill to high.

2. Combine Dijon mustard and soft brown sugar.

3. Season sirloin steaks generously with freshly ground black pepper.

4. Brush rack of grill pan with olive oil and place steaks on rack. Grill under preheated grill, 7.5 cm/3 in from heat, for 3 minutes on each side for rare steaks, 4 minutes on each side for medium, and 5 minutes on each side for well done, spreading with mustard and sugar mixture when you turn steaks over. Serve immediately.

Serves 4

Grilled Lamb Chops

8–12 (100-g/4-oz) loin of lamb chops,
  each 2.5 cm/1 in thick
lemon juice
dried rosemary or oregano
freshly ground black pepper
olive oil

1.　Preheat grill to high.

2.　Sprinkle lamb chops with lemon juice and dried rosemary or oregano, and season to taste with freshly ground black pepper.

3.　Brush rack of grill pan with olive oil. Place chops on rack and grill under preheated grill, 7.5 cm/3 in from heat, for 4 minutes on each side for a pink chop and 6 minutes on each side for a well-done chop. Serve immediately.

Serves 4 to 6

Grilled Lamb Chops with Lemon Mint Dressing

6 (100-g/4-oz) loin of lamb chops, each
  2.5 cm/1 in thick
3 tablespoons lemon juice
1 teaspoon grated lemon rind
2–3 tablespoons finely chopped mint
freshly ground black pepper
olive oil
1 clove garlic, finely chopped

1.　Season lamb chops generously with freshly ground black pepper.

2.　Combine lemon juice, 3 tablespoons olive oil, finely chopped mint, grated lemon rind and finely chopped garlic. Use to flavour chops. Reserve dressing.

3.　Brush rack of charcoal grill with olive oil. Place chops on rack and grill over hot charcoal, 10 cm/4 in from heat, for 5 minutes on each side for a pink chop and 7 minutes on each side for a well-done chop, basting occasionally with reserved dressing. Serve immediately.

Serves 3

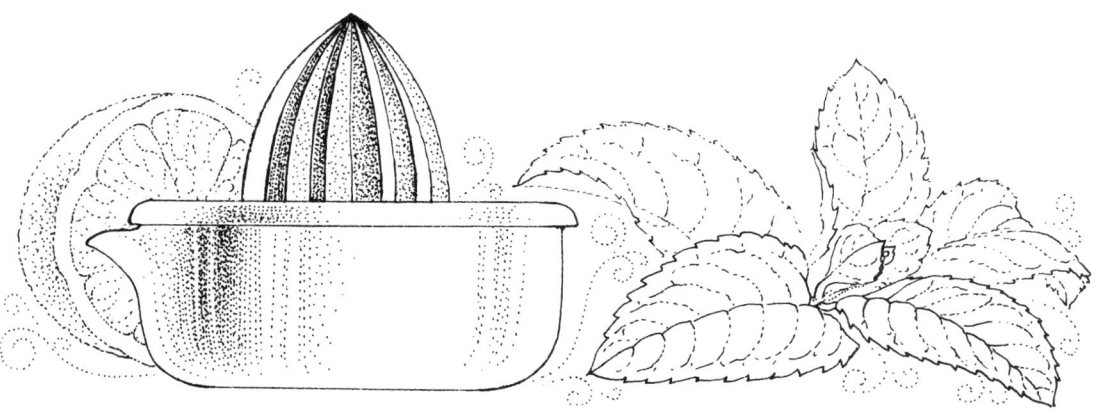

Gigot Steaks

4 leg of lamb steaks, each 2.5 cm/1 in
  thick
olive oil
1 clove garlic, finely chopped
2 bay leaves, crumbled
salt and freshly ground black pepper

1.   Preheat grill to high.

2.   Combine 6 tablespoons olive oil, finely
chopped garlic and crumbled bay leaves, and
season to taste with salt and freshly ground
black pepper.

3.   Marinate leg steaks in dressing for 10
minutes. Drain. Reserve dressing.

4.   Brush rack of grill pan with olive oil and
place steaks on rack. Grill under preheated
grill, 10 cm/4 in from heat, for 4 minutes on
each side for a pink steak and 6 minutes on each
side for a well-done steak, basting frequently
with reserved dressing during cooking. Serve
immediately.

Serves 4

Lamburgers

675 g/1½ lb boned leg of lamb, minced
1½ tablespoons single cream
2 tablespoons fresh breadcrumbs
1 tablespoon finely chopped chives
¼ teaspoon grated lemon rind
½ teaspoon paprika
¼ teaspoon cayenne
salt and freshly ground black pepper
melted butter
olive oil
1 x recipe quantity Béarnaise Sauce (page
55)

1.   Preheat grill to high.

2.   Combine minced lamb, single cream,
breadcrumbs, finely chopped chives and grated
lemon rind, and season with paprika, cayenne,
and salt and freshly ground black pepper to
taste. Form into four patties measuring
7.5 × 13 × 2.5 cm/3 × 5 × 1 in. Brush with
melted butter.

3.   Brush rack of grill pan with olive oil. Place
lamburgers on rack and grill under preheated
grill, 10 cm/4 in from heat, for 2 to 3 minutes
on each side for pink lamburgers, 4 to 5
minutes on each side for medium, and 6 to 7
minutes on each side for well done. Serve
immediately, accompanied by Béarnaise Sauce.

Serves 4

Snack Sausages with Cumberland Sauce

2 (227-g/8-oz) cans cocktail sausages, drained
3–4 tablespoons melted butter

CUMBERLAND SAUCE
225 g/8 oz redcurrant jelly
4 tablespoons Dijon mustard
1 tablespoon finely grated orange rind
6 tablespoons port, reduced to 2 tablespoons
cayenne

1. Preheat grill to high.

2. To make Cumberland Sauce, combine redcurrant jelly, Dijon mustard, finely grated orange rind and reduced port, and season to taste with cayenne. Pass through a fine sieve.

3. Thread 6 to 8 sausages on to each of eight metal skewers. Place in a buttered ovenproof gratin dish and brush with melted butter. Grill under preheated grill for 5 minutes, turning once and brushing with more melted butter. Pour over Cumberland Sauce and continue to cook for a further 10 minutes, basting once or twice. Transfer two skewers to each of four individual heated serving plates, spoon over sauce and serve immediately.

Serves 4

Liver and Bacon Kebabs

675 g/1½ lb calf's liver, cut into 32 even-sized cubes
24 rashers bacon, folded into quarters
olive oil
2 tablespoons lemon juice
1 medium-sized onion, finely chopped
bay leaf, crumbled
2 drops Tabasco sauce
salt and freshly ground black pepper

1. Preheat grill to high.

2. Combine 6 tablespoons olive oil, lemon juice, finely chopped onion, crumbled bay leaf and Tabasco, and season to taste with salt and freshly ground black pepper. Use to flavour liver cubes. Reserve dressing.

3. Thread liver cubes on to eight metal skewers, alternating them with bacon quarters. Brush with reserved dressing.

4. Brush rack of grill pan with olive oil and place kebabs on rack. Grill under preheated grill, 13 cm/5 in from heat, for 10 to 15 minutes, or until bacon is crisp and liver is browned, turning frequently. Serve immediately.

Serves 4

Chinese Skewered Beef with Oyster and Soy Sauce

675 g–1 kg/1½–2 lb sirloin of beef, cut into
even-sized cubes
thin slices of preserved ginger
olive oil
2 spring onions, cut into 5-mm/¼-in
pieces

OYSTER AND SOY SAUCE
1 tablespoon Chinese oyster sauce
1 tablespoon soy sauce
1 tablespoon liquid honey
2 tablespoons dry white wine
2 tablespoons peanut oil
2 tablespoons finely chopped onion
cayenne, chilli sauce or Tabasco sauce

1. Preheat grill to high.

2. To make Oyster and Soy Sauce, combine
first six ingredients and season to taste with
cayenne, chilli sauce or Tabasco.

3. Flavour beef cubes with sauce. Reserve
sauce.

4. Thread beef cubes on to eight metal
skewers, placing a thin slice of preserved
ginger between every two or three cubes.
Brush with reserved sauce.

5. Brush rack of grill pan with olive oil and
place skewers on rack. Grill under preheated
grill, 7.5 cm/3 in from heat, for 2 minutes for
rare beef, 3 to 4 minutes for medium, and 5 to 6
minutes for well done, turning frequently and
basting with reserved sauce. Serve, scattered
with spring onion pieces.

Serves 4

Quick and Easy Party Kebabs

Chinese Prawn Kebabs

Skewer 2 peeled cooked prawns. Marinate in
Oyster and Soy Sauce (left) for 10 minutes.
Drain. Grill under preheated grill for 1 to 2
minutes on each side. Delicious!

Mini Shish Kebabs

Arrange cubes of lamb, pieces of red or green
pepper, button onions and button mushrooms
on skewers. Marinate for 10 minutes in an olive
oil and lemon juice dressing, made as follows:
combine 4 tablespoons each of olive oil and
lemon juice, 2 tablespoons finely chopped
parsley, 2 crumbled bay leaves and a little finely
chopped onion or garlic, and season to taste
with salt and freshly ground black pepper.
Drain skewers. Grill under preheated grill for 8
to 10 minutes, turning frequently.

Pigs in a Blanket

The 'blanket' is bacon! Wrap small chipolata
sausages in half a rasher of bacon. Skewer and
grill under preheated grill for 8 to 10 minutes,
turning frequently. Before serving, dip in a
mustard sauce (made by combining 2 teaspoons Dijon mustard and 2 tablespoons
double cream).

Chicken Wing Tips

Cut baby chicken wings at joints. Marinate for
10 minutes in Oyster and Soy Sauce (left).
Drain. Reserve marinade sauce. Skewer wings
with bacon-wrapped banana rounds and grill
under preheated grill for 4 to 5 minutes,
turning and basting with marinade sauce
frequently.

CONTINUED ON PAGE 98

QUICK AND EASY PARTY KEBABS CONTINUED

Orange Segment, Ham and Olive Roll-Ups

Arrange orange segments, cubes of cooked ham and stuffed green olives on skewers. Brush with olive oil, sprinkle with brown sugar and grill under preheated grill for 2 to 3 minutes, turning frequently.

Mexican Meatball Kebabs

Combine 225 g/8 oz minced lamb or beef, 1 finely chopped small onion and 1 tablespoon finely chopped parsley. Season with $\frac{1}{4}$ teaspoon each ground cumin and cayenne, and salt and freshly ground black pepper to taste. Add 1 beaten egg. Form mixture into small balls and stuff them into poached and cored courgette chunks, hollowed-out canned button onions and, if available, hollowed-out baby tomatoes. Skewer, brush with olive oil and grill under preheated grill for 10 minutes on each side.

Note Use any extra Mexican meatball mixture, pan-fried, as cocktail snacks.

Chocolate Fondue Kebabs

A dipping dessert kebab! Melt 15 g/$\frac{1}{2}$ oz butter, 100 g/4 oz bitter chocolate and 1 tablespoon soured cream. Add 1 tablespoon cognac or coffee-flavoured liqueur. Guests dip fruits—pineapple chunks, strawberries, cherries—into hot sauce.

Charcoal-Grilled Beef or Pork Roast

675 g/1$\frac{1}{2}$ lb cold rare roast beef or cold roast pork, in one piece
olive oil

BARBECUE SAUCE
1 (50-g/1$\frac{3}{4}$-oz) can anchovy fillets, drained
2 egg yolks
2–3 teaspoons Dijon mustard
2–3 teaspoons tomato purée
4 tablespoons olive oil
1 teaspoon Worcestershire sauce
cayenne
freshly ground black pepper

1. To make Barbecue Sauce, place anchovy fillets in a mortar and pound to a smooth paste. Add egg yolks, Dijon mustard and tomato purée. Beat in olive oil and Worcestershire sauce. Season with a little cayenne and freshly ground black pepper.

2. Cut rare roast beef or roast pork into 16 even-sized fingers and brush liberally with sauce.

3. Brush rack of charcoal grill with olive oil and place beef or pork fingers on rack. Grill over hot charcoal for 10 minutes, or until golden brown on all sides. Serve immediately.

Serves 4

Quick and Easy Party Kebabs (page 97 and above)

Chicken with Chinese Dressing

2 small frying chickens, quartered
2 tablespoons soy sauce
2 tablespoons Chinese oyster sauce
olive oil
1 tablespoon dry white wine
4 tablespoons finely chopped parsley
freshly ground black pepper

1.   Preheat grill to high.

2.   Combine soy sauce, Chinese oyster sauce, 2 tablespoons olive oil, dry white wine and finely chopped parsley, and season to taste with freshly ground black pepper. Flavour chicken quarters with dressing. Reserve dressing.

3.   Brush rack of grill pan with olive oil and place chicken leg quarters, fleshy side up, on rack. Grill under preheated grill, 13 cm/5 in from heat, for 5 minutes.

4.   Place chicken breast quarters on rack and turn legs. Brush all pieces with reserved dressing and continue to grill for a further 15 minutes, turning and basting with reserved dressing once more. Serve immediately.

Serves 8

Lemon-Grilled Baby Chicken

2 small frying chickens, quartered
salt and freshly ground black pepper
olive oil

LEMON BARBECUE SAUCE
150 ml/$\frac{1}{4}$ pint olive oil
6 tablespoons lemon juice
3 tablespoons finely chopped onion
1–2 teaspoons dried tarragon
1–2 teaspoons finely chopped parsley
salt and freshly ground black pepper
Tabasco sauce

1.   Preheat grill to high.

2.   To make Lemon Barbecue Sauce, combine first five ingredients and season to taste with salt, freshly ground black pepper and Tabasco.

3.   Generously season chicken quarters with salt and freshly ground black pepper and brush liberally with sauce. Reserve sauce.

4.   Brush rack of grill pan with olive oil and place chicken legs, fleshy side up, on rack. Grill under preheated grill, 13 cm/5 in from heat, for 5 minutes.

5.   Place chicken breasts on rack and turn legs. Brush all pieces with reserved sauce and continue to grill for a further 15 minutes, turning and basting with reserved sauce once more. Serve immediately.

Serves 8

Devilled Chicken Legs

4 cooked chicken legs (drumsticks and
 thighs)
melted butter
2 teaspoons prepared English mustard
2 teaspoons French mustard
1 teaspoon curry paste
2 teaspoons mango chutney
pinch of cayenne
salt and freshly ground black pepper
olive oil

1.   Preheat grill to high.

2.   Score flesh fairly deeply along and across
chicken pieces and brush with melted butter.

3.   Combine mustards, curry paste and mango
chutney, and season with cayenne, and salt and
freshly ground black pepper to taste. Spread
mixture over chicken pieces.

4.   Brush rack of grill pan with olive oil and
place chicken pieces on rack. Grill under
preheated grill, 7.5 cm/3 in from heat, for 5 to 7
minutes on each side, basting with remaining
melted butter from time to time. Serve
immediately.

Serves 4

Devilled Duck Legs

6 cooked duck legs (drumsticks and
 thighs)
75 g/3 oz butter
1 teaspoon mustard powder
1 tablespoon curry powder
2 teaspoons caster sugar
$\frac{1}{2}$ teaspoon salt
$\frac{1}{2}$ teaspoon paprika
1 teaspoon Worcestershire sauce
freshly ground black pepper
olive oil

1.   Preheat grill to high.

2.   Score flesh fairly deeply along and across
duck pieces.

3.   Melt butter in a thick-bottomed saucepan,
stir in the next six ingredients and season to
taste with freshly ground black pepper. Brush
both sides of duck pieces generously with the
mixture. Reserve mixture.

4.   Brush rack of grill pan with olive oil and
place duck pieces on rack. Grill under preheated grill, 7.5 cm/3 in from heat, for 5 to 7
minutes on each side, basting with reserved
mixture from time to time. Serve immediately.

Serves 6

CHAPTER EIGHT

OUT OF THE FRYING PAN

Chinese Steak with Green Pepper

450 g/1 lb lean sirloin or rump steak
1 green pepper, deseeded and diced
4 tablespoons peanut oil
1 small clove garlic
1 small onion, diced
$\frac{1}{4}$ teaspoon ground ginger
salt and freshly ground black pepper
1 tablespoon cornflour
150 ml/$\frac{1}{4}$ pint chicken stock (made with $\frac{1}{2}$ chicken stock cube)
1–2 teaspoons soy sauce

1.   Cut sirloin or rump steak diagonally across the grain into thin slices, and then into strips about 5 cm/2 in long.

2.   Heat peanut oil in a wok or thick-bottomed frying pan. Place garlic in hot oil for 3 minutes. Remove from pan with a slotted spoon and discard.

3.   Add steak strips to wok or pan and sauté until steak strips just begin to brown. Add diced pepper and onion and ground ginger, and season to taste with salt and freshly ground black pepper. Continue to cook, stirring constantly, for a further 3 to 5 minutes, or until vegetables are just tender.

4.   Combine cornflour, chicken stock and soy sauce.

5.   Stir cornflour mixture into wok or pan and bring to the boil. Cook, stirring constantly, until liquids thicken. Transfer to a heated serving platter and serve immediately.

Serves 4

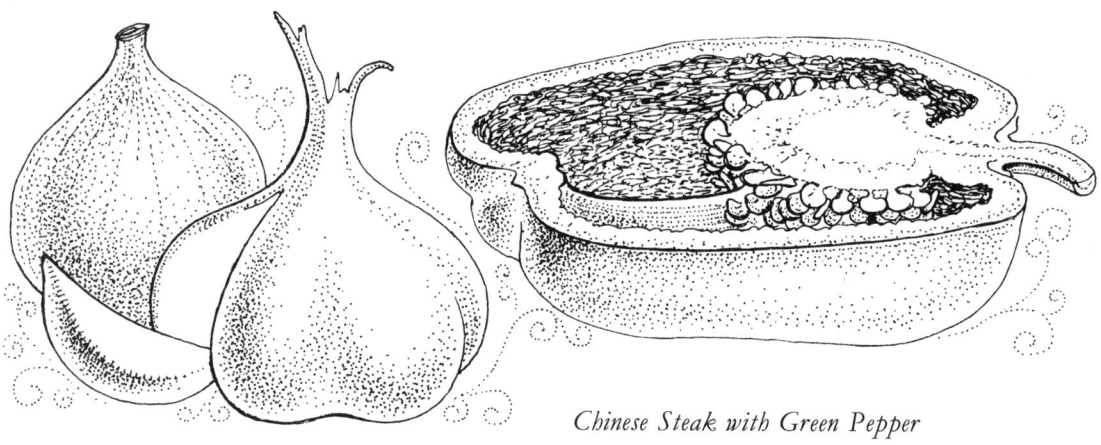

Chinese Steak with Green Pepper

Stir-Fried Chicken

2 chicken breasts, cut into matchstick-
sized strips
1 teaspoon cornflour
1 teaspoon soy sauce
1 clove garlic, finely chopped
5 tablespoons peanut oil
4 small onions, cut into thin rings
1 small head celery, cut into matchstick-
sized strips
1 green pepper, deseeded and cut into
matchstick-sized strips
1 (227-g/8-oz) can water chestnuts,
drained and halved
225 g/8 oz French beans, halved
1 tablespoon dry white wine
salt and freshly ground black pepper

1. Dilute cornflour in soy sauce and 2
tablespoons water. Add finely chopped garlic.
Toss chicken strips in marinade and allow to
stand for 10 minutes. Drain.

2. Meanwhile, heat 2 tablespoons peanut oil
in a wok or thick-bottomed frying pan and stir-
fry onion rings until just golden brown. Add
celery and green pepper strips, halved water
chestnuts and French beans, and dry white
wine. Cover and simmer until vegetables are
just tender. Season to taste with salt and freshly
ground black pepper.

3. Heat remaining peanut oil in another wok
or pan and stir-fry chicken strips, stirring
constantly, until golden brown on all sides.

4. Combine chicken strips and vegetables,
transfer to a heated serving platter and serve
immediately.

Serves 4 to 6

Pork and Prawn Chow Mein

175 g/6 oz cooked pork, in one piece, cut
into thin strips
100 g/4 oz cooked prawns, peeled
2 tablespoons peanut oil
1 medium-sized onion, finely chopped
1 small head celery, finely chopped
300 ml/½ pint chicken stock (made with ¾
chicken stock cube)
1 teaspoon salt
freshly ground black pepper
175 g/6 oz bean sprouts
lettuce leaves
sliced spring onions
1 Chinese Omelette (page 65), cut into
thin strips

FLAVOURING AND THICKENING INGREDIENTS
2 tablespoons cornflour
1–2 tablespoons soy sauce
1 teaspoon sugar

1. Heat peanut oil in a wok or thick-
bottomed frying pan and sauté finely chopped
onion and celery until soft but not coloured.
Add chicken stock and salt, and season to taste
with freshly ground black pepper. Cover and
cook for 5 minutes, or until just tender.

2. Add pork strips, peeled cooked prawns
and bean sprouts to wok or pan. Continue to
cook until heated through. Meanwhile, combine flavouring and thickening ingredients
with 2 tablespoons water.

3. Add mixture to wok or pan and bring to
the boil. Cook, stirring constantly, until liquids
thicken. Transfer to a heated serving platter
and garnish with lettuce leaves, sliced spring
onions and strips of Chinese Omelette.

Serves 4

Sweet-and-Sour Meatballs

450 g/1 lb lean sirloin or rump steak,
  minced
soy sauce
Tabasco sauce
2 spring onions, finely chopped
1 egg, lightly beaten
2 tablespoons flour
salt and freshly ground black pepper
4 tablespoons peanut oil
2 green peppers, deseeded and diced
1 (227-g/8-oz) can pineapple slices,
  drained and diced, 6 tablespoons juice
  reserved from can
150 ml/¼ pint chicken stock
6 tablespoons dry white wine

FLAVOURING AND THICKENING INGREDIENTS
2 tablespoons cornflour
1 tablespoon soy sauce
6 tablespoons red wine vinegar
6 tablespoons sugar

1. Season minced sirloin or rump steak to taste with soy sauce and Tabasco. Combine with finely chopped spring onion and form into 16 small balls.

2. Combine lightly beaten egg and flour to make a batter. Season to taste with salt and freshly ground black pepper.

3. Heat peanut oil in a wok or thick-bottomed frying pan. Dip meatballs in batter, draining carefully, and sauté them until golden brown on all sides. Keep warm.

4. Pour off all but 1 tablespoon oil from wok or pan, then sauté diced green peppers and pineapple in remaining oil until soft but not coloured. Add chicken stock and dry white wine. Cover and cook for 5 minutes, or until peppers and pineapple are just tender.

5. Meanwhile, combine flavouring and thickening ingredients and reserved pineapple juice.

6. Add flavouring and thickening ingredients to wok or pan. Bring to the boil and cook, stirring constantly, until liquids thicken. Add meatballs and heat through. Transfer to a heated serving platter and serve immediately.

Serves 4

Japanese Braised Pork with Cucumbers

2 small pork fillets, each cut crossways
  into 3 even-sized pieces
2 cucumbers
6 spring onions, green parts only
peanut oil
225 g/8 oz mange-tout peas, or a selection
  of fresh vegetables of your choice
2 tablespoons white wine vinegar
1–2 teaspoons salt
2 teaspoons sugar

BRAISING SAUCE
6 tablespoons soy sauce
6 tablespoons sake or a mixture of dry
  sherry and water
2 teaspoons sugar

1. Place each pork fillet piece between two sheets of wet cling film and beat into thin rectangles.

2. Cut each cucumber into 3 even-sized lengths, and then cut each length into 3 strips. Place strips in a thick-bottomed saucepan, cover with cold water and bring to the boil. Drain on absorbent kitchen paper.

3. Cut green parts of spring onions to the same length as cucumber strips.

4. Place 3 cucumber strips and 4 spring onion strips on each rectangle of pork. Wrap pork round vegetables and secure with wooden cocktail sticks.

5. Pour peanut oil to a depth of 1 cm/$\frac{1}{2}$ in into a thick-bottomed frying pan large enough to take pork and cucumber rolls in one layer. Heat. Place rolls in pan and cook over a high heat for 2 minutes, or until golden brown, turning frequently.

6. Meanwhile, combine braising sauce ingredients.

7. Pour off excess oil from pan and pour in braising sauce ingredients. Simmer pork and cucumber rolls for 6 to 7 minutes, or until tender, turning frequently. Remove from pan with a slotted spoon. Remove cocktail sticks and cut each roll into 3 even-sized pieces. Keep warm.

8. Meanwhile, blanch mange-tout peas, or other fresh vegetables, in boiling water. Drain on absorbent kitchen paper. Place in a shallow dish, sprinkle with a mixture of white wine vinegar, salt and sugar, and allow to marinate for a few minutes. Drain and keep warm.

9. Cook sauce remaining in pan until reduced to a thick glaze.

10. To serve: spoon a little sauce to cover the bottom of six individual serving plates. Stand 3 pork and cucumber rolls on each plate. Garnish with mange-tout peas, or other vegetables, and serve immediately.

Serves 6

Japanese Braised Pork with Cucumbers

Chinese Batter-Dipped Pork

1 small pork fillet, cut into thin strips
1 small egg, well beaten
2 teaspoons soy sauce
1 teaspoon dry sherry
$\frac{1}{4}$ teaspoon salt
$\frac{1}{2}$ teaspoon monosodium glutamate
75 g/3 oz flour
oil for deep frying

1. Combine well-beaten egg, soy sauce, dry sherry and 1 teaspoon water in a shallow dish.

2. Combine salt, monosodium glutamate and flour in a paper bag.

3. Dip pork strips into egg mixture, draining carefully, and place in paper bag. Shake until evenly coated. Remove from bag, shaking off excess flour.

4. Heat oil in a wok or deep-fryer to a temperature of 190 C, 375 F; a 2.5-cm/1-in cube of day-old bread takes 1 minute to turn crisp and golden brown at this temperature.

5. Deep-fry pork strips in preheated oil for 6 to 8 minutes, or until golden brown. Drain on absorbent kitchen paper. Transfer to a heated serving platter and serve immediately.

Serves 2

Chinese Batter-Dipped Pork with Pineapple and Green Pepper

1 x recipe quantity Chinese Batter-Dipped Pork (left)
1 (227-g/8-oz) can pineapple chunks, drained, 6 tablespoons pineapple juice reserved
1 medium-sized green pepper, deseeded and cut into 1-cm/$\frac{1}{2}$-in dice
1 tablespoon peanut oil
1 medium-sized onion, cut into 1-cm/$\frac{1}{2}$-in dice
4 tablespoons chicken stock

FLAVOURING AND THICKENING INGREDIENTS
2 teaspoons cornflour
1 teaspoon soy sauce
2 tablespoons sugar
1 teaspoon tomato ketchup

1. Heat peanut oil in a wok or thick-bottomed frying pan and lightly toss pineapple chunks and diced green pepper and onion until onion is soft but not coloured. Add chicken stock, cover and cook for 2 to 3 minutes, or until vegetables are just tender.

2. Add Chinese Batter-Dipped Pork to wok or pan and continue to cook, uncovered, until pork is heated through.

3. Meanwhile, combine flavouring and thickening ingredients and reserved pineapple juice.

4. Add flavouring and thickening ingredients to wok or pan. Bring to the boil and cook, stirring constantly, until the liquids thicken. Transfer to a heated serving platter and serve immediately.

Serves 2

Veal Steaks in Pizza Sauce

4 thin veal steaks
4 tablespoons olive oil
1 or 2 cloves garlic, finely chopped
salt and freshly ground black pepper
1 (397-g/14-oz) can peeled Italian
   tomatoes
1 teaspoon sugar
12 stuffed olives, sliced
½–1 teaspoon dried oregano
1 tablespoon finely chopped parsley

1.   Heat olive oil in a thick-bottomed frying pan, add finely chopped garlic and veal steaks and sauté veal steaks for 1 minute on each side. Remove from pan with a slotted spoon. Season to taste with salt and freshly ground black pepper. Keep warm.

2.   Add canned tomatoes and sugar to pan and cook for 10 to 15 minutes. Season to taste with salt and freshly ground black pepper.

3.   Add sliced olives, dried oregano and finely chopped parsley and continue to cook for a further 5 minutes, or until smooth and well blended.

4.   Return veal steaks to pan and continue to cook until veal steaks are tender but still pink. Transfer to a heated serving dish and serve immediately.

Serves 4

Italian Sauté of Veal with Sage

4 slices veal
8–12 small sage leaves, or dried sage
salt and freshly ground black pepper
8–12 thin slices mozzarella cheese
flour
40 g/1½ oz butter
2 tablespoons Marsala or dry white wine

1.   Place each veal slice between two sheets of cling film and beat with a meat bat into thin rectangles. Cut each rectangle into two or three even-sized slices.

2.   Place 1 sage leaf, or a pinch of dried sage, on each slice of veal and season to taste with salt and freshly ground black pepper. Cover with 1 mozzarella cheese slice. Form into a small roll and secure with wooden cocktail sticks. Dust with flour.

3.   Melt butter in a thick-bottomed frying pan and sauté veal rolls until golden brown, turning frequently.

4.   Add Marsala or dry white wine to pan. Cover and simmer for 2 to 3 minutes, or until veal rolls are tender. Transfer to a heated serving platter, remove cocktail sticks and serve immediately.

Serves 4

Italian Crumbed Veal

8 slices veal
flour
salt and freshly ground black pepper
cayenne
2 eggs, well beaten
4 tablespoons fresh breadcrumbs
100 g/4 oz freshly grated Parmesan cheese
25 g/1 oz butter
2 tablespoons olive oil

1.   Place each veal slice between two sheets of wet cling film and beat flat with a meat bat.

2.   Place flour in a shallow dish and season generously with salt, freshly ground black pepper and a hint of cayenne. Pour well-beaten eggs into another dish. Combine breadcrumbs and freshly grated Parmesan cheese in a third dish.

3.   Dip veal slices in seasoned flour, shaking off excess, then dip slices in well-beaten eggs, draining carefully, and finally roll them in breadcrumb and cheese mixture, patting coating on firmly.

4.   Melt butter with olive oil in a thick-bottomed frying pan and sauté veal slices on both sides until golden brown. Transfer to a heated serving platter and serve immediately.

Serves 8

Calf's Liver with Sherry Vinegar

12 thin slices calf's liver
2 tablespoons dry sherry
1 tablespoon red wine vinegar
flour
salt and freshly ground black pepper
cayenne
175 g/6 oz butter
juice of $\frac{1}{2}$ lemon
$\frac{1}{4}$ teaspoon dried thyme

1.   Place flour in a shallow dish and season it generously with salt, freshly ground black pepper and a hint of cayenne.

2.   Dip calf's liver slices in seasoned flour, shaking off excess.

3.   Melt 50 g/2 oz butter in a thick-bottomed frying pan and sauté liver slices for 30 seconds on each side. Using a slotted spoon, transfer slices from pan to a heated serving platter. Keep warm.

4.   Add dry sherry and red wine vinegar to pan and cook over a high heat until reduced to a glaze, stirring in all the crusty bits from bottom and sides of pan. Reserve.

5.   Melt remaining butter in a thick-bottomed saucepan. Add reserved pan juices, lemon juice and dried thyme and bring to the boil. Strain sauce over liver slices and serve immediately.

Serves 6

Pan-Fried Liver Brochettes with Sage

575 g/1¼ lb calf's liver, cut into even-sized
  cubes
24 sage leaves
salt and freshly ground black pepper
cayenne
40 g/1½ oz butter
2 tablespoons olive oil
1 medium-sized onion, finely chopped

1.   Thread calf's liver cubes on to eight metal skewers, alternating cubes with sage leaves. Season to taste with salt, freshly ground black pepper and cayenne.

2.   Melt butter with olive oil in a thick-bottomed frying pan and sauté finely chopped onion until soft but not coloured.

3.   Add liver brochettes to pan and pan-fry for 2 to 3 minutes on each side, or until liver is brown and tender. Transfer to a heated serving platter and serve immediately.

Serves 4

Calf's Liver with Bacon

4 thin slices calf's liver
4 thin rashers streaky bacon
flour
salt and freshly ground black pepper
50 g/2 oz butter
sprigs of parsley

GREEN BUTTER
50 g/2 oz softened butter
1 clove garlic, crushed
1 tablespoon finely chopped parsley
1 tablespoon lemon juice
salt and freshly ground black pepper

1.   To make Green Butter, combine softened butter, crushed garlic and finely chopped parsley, and season with lemon juice, and salt and freshly ground black pepper to taste. Shape butter into a neat roll and wrap tightly in cling film. Chill until firm. Cut into four even-sized rounds.

2.   Meanwhile, place flour in a shallow dish and season generously with salt and freshly ground black pepper.

3.   Dip calf's liver slices in seasoned flour, shaking off excess.

4.   Melt butter in a thick-bottomed frying pan and sauté bacon rashers until crisp. Remove from pan with a slotted spoon. Drain on absorbent kitchen paper. Keep warm.

5.   Sauté liver slices in fats remaining in pan for 30 seconds on each side. Transfer to a heated serving platter and cover each slice with a rasher of bacon. Top with a round of Green Butter, garnish with parsley sprigs and serve.

Serves 4

Southern Fried Chicken

1 (1.5-kg/3½-lb) chicken
salt and freshly ground white pepper
flour
lard for deep frying (see note below)
finely chopped parsley

SAUCE
25 g/1 oz butter
25 g/1 oz flour
150 ml/¼ pint milk
150 ml/¼ pint single cream
salt and freshly ground white pepper

1. Cut chicken into serving pieces and season to taste with salt and freshly ground white pepper.

2. Place flour in a shallow dish and season generously with salt and freshly ground white pepper. Toss chicken pieces in seasoned flour, shaking off excess.

3. Melt lard in a large thick-bottomed frying pan; the lard should be at a minimum depth of 5 cm/2 in. When lard is hot but not smoking, add chicken pieces. Cover and cook over a low heat for 10 minutes. Remove lid, increase heat and continue cooking for a further 10 to 15 minutes, or until golden brown. Drain on absorbent kitchen paper.

4. Meanwhile, prepare sauce. Melt butter in a thick-bottomed saucepan, add flour and cook for 2 to 3 minutes, stirring constantly, until flour is cooked through. Gradually add milk and continue cooking, stirring vigorously, until thick and smooth. Add single cream, season to taste with salt and freshly ground white pepper, and continue cooking until hot but not boiling.

5. Transfer chicken pieces to a heated serving dish, pour over a little sauce and garnish with parsley. Serve immediately, accompanied by remaining sauce, Corn Fritters (below) and Fried Bananas (page 114).

Serves 4

Note   Lard is the traditional, flavourful frying agent in Southern country cooking. If you prefer a lighter medium, use peanut oil.

Corn Fritters

1 (340-g/12-oz) can sweet corn, drained
3 tablespoons finely chopped onion
2 eggs, well beaten
100 g/4 oz flour
1 teaspoon baking powder
2 teaspoons sugar
¾ teaspoon salt
2 tablespoons melted butter
150 ml/¼ pint milk
olive oil

1. Combine sweet corn, onion and eggs.

2. Sift together flour, baking powder, sugar and salt.

3. Blend melted butter, milk and flour mixture into sweet corn and onion mixture.

4. Lightly oil and heat a griddle or a cast-iron frying pan. Spoon a small ladleful of batter (2 to 3 tablespoons) on to griddle or into pan. Pat into shape. When underside is firm, turn and cook until golden brown.

Makes 8 to 12

Southern Fried Chicken with Corn Fritters and Fried Bananas (above and page 114)

Fried Bananas

8 small bananas
lemon juice
25 g/1 oz butter
juice and finely grated rind of 1 orange
25 g/1 oz caster sugar

1. Peel bananas. Brush with lemon juice to preserve colour and allow to stand for a few minutes to absorb lemon flavour.

2. Meanwhile, melt butter in a thick-bottomed frying pan large enough to take bananas side by side. Add orange juice and finely grated rind, and caster sugar, and stir over a low heat until sugar has dissolved.

3. Arrange bananas in pan and brown on all sides, taking care not to burn sauce or overcook bananas.

Makes 8

Chicken Scallopini with Lemon

2 boned chicken breasts
juice of $\frac{1}{2}$ lemon
salt and freshly ground black pepper
50 g/2 oz butter
2 tablespoons olive oil
1 Spanish onion, coarsely chopped
1 clove garlic, finely chopped
6 tablespoons Madeira
150 ml/$\frac{1}{4}$ pint double cream
4–6 tablespoons coarsely chopped almonds
4–6 slices lemon

1. Cut chicken breasts diagonally across the grain into slices 5 mm/$\frac{1}{4}$ in thick. Season generously with salt and freshly ground black pepper.

2. Melt the butter with the olive oil in a thick-bottomed frying pan and sauté coarsely chopped onion and finely chopped garlic until soft but not coloured. Remove from pan with a slotted spoon. Keep warm.

3. Sauté chicken slices in remaining fat until golden brown on all sides.

4. Return vegetables to pan. Stir once. Add Madeira and cook over a high heat until Madeira has reduced to half its original quantity.

5. Add lemon juice and double cream to pan, lower heat and cook until sauce is hot but not boiling. Transfer to a heated serving platter. Garnish with coarsely chopped almonds and lemon slices and serve immediately.

Serves 4 to 6

Pan-Fried Pepper Steak

4 (100 to 175-g/4 to 6-oz) fillet steaks,
  each 4 cm/1½ in thick
2 tablespoons crushed black peppercorns
salt
40 g/1½ oz butter
1 tablespoon olive oil
dash of cognac
6 tablespoons beef stock
2 tablespoons double cream

1.   Beat fillet steaks on each side with a meat bat, to tenderise meat. Season to taste with salt, and press crushed black peppercorns into each side.

2.   Melt 25 g/1 oz butter with the olive oil in a thick-bottomed frying pan and pan-fry steaks over a high heat for 2 minutes on each side. Reduce heat and continue to pan-fry for a further 4 minutes on each side for rare steaks, 7 to 8 minutes on each side for medium, and 9 to 10 minutes on each side for well done. Transfer steaks from pan with a slotted spoon to a heated serving platter. Keep warm.

3.   Add cognac and beef stock to the pan and cook over a high heat until liquid has reduced to half its original quantity.

4.   Add remaining butter to pan and shake vigorously until butter is amalgamated into sauce. Add double cream and continue to shake pan until sauce is thick and smooth. Pour over steaks and serve immediately.

Serves 4

Quick Beef Stroganoff

450 g/1 lb beef fillet
50 g/2 oz butter
salt and freshly ground black pepper
paprika
4 tablespoons beef stock
1 tablespoon brandy
1 tablespoon dry sherry
150 ml/¼ pint soured cream
lemon juice

1.   Cut beef fillet diagonally across the grain into slices 5 mm/¼ in thick, and then into strips 5 cm/2 in long.

2.   Melt butter in a thick-bottomed frying pan and sauté beef slices for 2 to 3 minutes, stirring constantly. Season to taste with salt, freshly ground black pepper and paprika. Add beef stock, cover and simmer for 2 to 3 minutes, or until beef is tender but still quite rare. Remove from pan with a slotted spoon. Keep warm.

3.   Add brandy and dry sherry to pan and cook over a high heat until liquid has reduced to half its original quantity.

4.   Lower heat, add soured cream to pan and sprinkle with lemon juice. Return beef slices and toss until sauce begins to bubble; do not allow sauce to come to the boil. Transfer to a heated serving platter and serve immediately.

Serves 4 to 6

Veal Medallions with Black Truffle

4 veal medallions, 2.5 cm/1 in thick
4 slices black truffle
salt and freshly ground black pepper
25 g/1 oz butter
2 tablespoons olive oil
6 tablespoons dry white wine or Madeira

TOMATO SAUCE
25 g/1 oz butter
2 tablespoons olive oil
1 medium-sized onion, finely chopped
1 stick celery, finely chopped
1 clove garlic, finely chopped
1 (227-g/8-oz) can peeled Italian
  tomatoes, chopped
2 teaspoons glace de viande (page 10)
150 ml/¼ pint double cream
dry white wine or light chicken stock
  (optional)
cayenne
lemon juice
salt and freshly ground black pepper

1.   To make Tomato Sauce, melt butter with olive oil in a thick-bottomed pan and sauté onion, celery and garlic until soft but not coloured. Add tomatoes and continue to cook, pressing tomatoes to the bottom and sides of pan, until sauce is relatively smooth. Add *glace de viande* and double cream, lower heat and simmer for 10 minutes; add a little water, wine or stock if sauce becomes too dry. Season with a hint of cayenne, and lemon juice, salt and freshly ground black pepper to taste.

2.   Meanwhile, season veal medallions generously with salt and freshly ground black pepper.

3.   Melt butter with olive oil in a thick-bottomed frying pan and sauté veal medallions for 3 to 4 minutes on each side; medallions should be moist and tender—not too cooked or they become tough. Remove from pan with a slotted spoon and keep warm.

4.   Pour off excess fats from pan and pour in wine or Madeira. Cook over a high heat, stirring in all the crusty bits from bottom and sides of pan, until liquid has reduced by half. Strain into the Tomato Sauce.

5.   Return veal medallions to pan. Place 1 slice black truffle on each medallion, strain sauce round medallions and serve immediately.

Serves 4

Veal Medallions with Black Truffle

Danish Meatballs

225 g/8 oz pork fillet, minced
225 g/8 oz veal fillet, minced
50 g/2 oz butter
1 medium-sized onion, finely chopped
4 tablespoons fresh breadcrumbs
1 egg
5 tablespoons milk
¼ teaspoon grated nutmeg
pinch of cayenne
salt and freshly ground black pepper
2 tablespoons olive oil

1.   Melt 25 g/1 oz butter in a frying pan and sauté onion until soft but not coloured.

2.   Combine onion, pork, veal, breadcrumbs, egg and milk, and season with grated nutmeg, cayenne, and salt and freshly ground black pepper to taste. Form into 16 small balls.

3.   Melt remaining butter with the olive oil in another pan and sauté meatballs until golden brown on all sides. Transfer to a heated serving dish and serve.

Serves 4

Sauté of Lamb with French Beans

1 rack of lamb, trimmed
225 g/8 oz cooked French beans, cut into 2.5-cm/1-in pieces
salt and freshly ground black pepper
bay leaf, crumbled
¼ chicken stock cube, crumbled
4 tablespoons olive oil
butter
2 tablespoons finely chopped parsley or chives

SAUCE
½ chicken stock cube
2 tablespoons tomato purée
1 medium-sized onion, finely chopped
bay leaf
4 tablespoons dry white wine
beurre manié (made by mashing 1 teaspoon each of flour and butter together to form a smooth paste)
salt and freshly ground black pepper

1.   Cut meat from bones of rack of lamb, making a fillet of lamb. Cut fillet into 2.5-cm/1-in slices. Reserve bones and trimmings for sauce.

2.   Cut each slice into three or four even-sized cubes. Place lamb cubes in an earthenware or porcelain (not metal) bowl and season generously with freshly ground black pepper. Add crumbled bay leaf, ¼ chicken stock cube and olive oil. Toss until lamb cubes are glistening. Allow to stand until ready to cook.

3.   To make sauce, coarsely chop reserved bones and place in a thick-bottomed saucepan. Add reserved trimmings, ½ chicken stock cube, tomato purée, finely chopped onion, bay leaf and dry white wine. Pour in enough water just to cover and cook until meat remaining on

bones is cooked through. Strain into a clean pan and cook over a high heat until reduced to half the original quantity. Whisk in *beurre manié* and season to taste with salt and freshly ground black pepper.

4.   Meanwhile, melt a little butter in a thick-bottomed frying pan and sauté French bean pieces until heated through. Season to taste with salt and freshly ground black pepper. Keep warm.

5.   Drain lamb cubes. Heat marinating oil in another pan and sauté lamb cubes until golden brown on all sides but still quite rare. Pour off excess oil. Add sauce and bring just to the boil. Stir in French bean pieces. Transfer to a heated serving dish, sprinkle with finely chopped parsley or chives and serve immediately.

Serves 4

Medallions of Lamb with Spinach and Lime

2 boned racks of lamb
450 g/1 lb spinach leaves
2 limes, divided into segments
salt and freshly ground black pepper
50 g/2 oz butter
5 tablespoons olive oil

LEMON AND CHIVE SAUCE
juice of 1 lemon
100 g/4 oz cold butter, diced
2 tablespoons finely chopped chives
salt and freshly ground black pepper

1.   Trim racks of lamb of all fat and tie into two neat rolls. Season generously with salt and freshly ground black pepper.

2.   Melt 25 g/1 oz butter with 2 tablespoons olive oil in a thick-bottomed frying pan and sauté lamb rolls for 4 to 6 minutes, or until well browned on all sides. Cut each roll in half and cut each half into three (1-cm/$\frac{1}{2}$-in) medallions.

3.   Wash spinach several times in cold water. Drain. Remove coarse stems and any damaged or yellowed leaves.

4.   Season medallions generously with salt and freshly ground black pepper.

5.   Melt remaining butter with 2 tablespoons olive oil in a thick-bottomed frying pan and sauté medallions for 3 minutes on each side.

6.   Meanwhile, heat remaining olive oil and 1 tablespoon water in a thick-bottomed saucepan. Add spinach leaves and cook for 1 to 2 minutes, or until leaves are just wilted. Season to taste with salt and freshly ground black pepper.

7.   Arrange wilted spinach on a heated serving platter, or on four individual heated serving plates, to serve as a colourful background for the medallions. Place lamb medallions down centre of platter, or plates, and garnish each side of medallions with lime segments. Keep warm.

8.   To make Lemon and Chive Sauce, deglaze pan with lemon juice and whisk in diced butter. Add finely chopped chives and season to taste with salt and freshly ground black pepper.

9.   Spoon sauce over medallions and serve immediately.

Serves 4

CHAPTER NINE

GRATINS AND CASSEROLES

Chicken Broccoli au Gratin

4 cooked chicken breasts, each cut into
  2 flat slices
1 (227-g/8-oz) packet frozen broccoli
  florets, defrosted
300 ml/$\frac{1}{2}$ pint Quick White Sauce (page
  49)
225 g/8 oz Gruyère cheese, freshly
  grated
1 large egg yolk
1 tablespoon double cream
salt and freshly ground black pepper
2 tablespoons freshly grated Parmesan
  cheese

1.   Preheat grill to high.

2.   Bring Quick White Sauce just to the boil.
Add grated Gruyère cheese and cook, stirring
occasionally, until melted. Meanwhile, prepare
broccoli according to packet directions.

3.   Combine egg yolk and double cream and
season to taste with salt and freshly ground
black pepper. Add to sauce.

4.   Place cooked broccoli in a heatproof gratin
dish, cover with chicken slices and mask with
sauce. Sprinkle with freshly grated Parmesan
cheese and brown under preheated grill. Serve
immediately, from the gratin dish.

Serves 4

Chicken à la King

350 g/12 oz cooked chicken, cut into
  4-cm/1$\frac{1}{2}$-in cubes
50 g/2 oz butter
3 tablespoons flour
450 ml/$\frac{3}{4}$ pint milk
1 medium-sized stick celery, sliced
50 g/2 oz button mushrooms, sliced
$\frac{1}{4}$ green pepper, deseeded and chopped
1 canned pimiento, chopped
salt and freshly ground black pepper
2 egg yolks
2 tablespoons double cream
1 tablespoon Worcestershire sauce
chopped parsley

1.   Melt 40 g/1$\frac{1}{2}$ oz butter, add flour and cook
for 2 to 3 minutes, stirring. Gradually add milk
and cook, stirring, until thick and smooth.

2.   Melt remaining butter and sauté sliced
celery and button mushrooms and chopped
pepper until soft but not coloured. Add celery,
mushrooms, pepper, chicken cubes and chopped pimiento to sauce and heat through.
Season to taste.

3.   Combine egg yolks, double cream and
Worcestershire sauce. Add to chicken mixture
and heat through. Transfer to a heated serving
dish, garnish with chopped parsley and serve.

Serves 6 to 8

Chicken à la King

Creamed Turkey

350 g/12 oz cooked turkey, diced
25 g/1 oz butter
2 tablespoons flour
½ chicken stock cube
300 ml/½ pint chicken stock, reduced to
  150 ml/¼ pint
300 ml/½ pint double cream
1 teaspoon finely chopped onion
½ teaspoon paprika
freshly ground black pepper
1–2 tablespoons dry sherry

1.   Melt butter in a thick-bottomed saucepan, add flour and cook for 2 to 3 minutes, stirring constantly, until flour is cooked through. Add the ½ chicken stock cube and reduced chicken stock and cook, stirring vigorously, until thick and smooth. Add double cream and heat through.

2.   Add diced turkey and finely chopped onion to pan. Season with paprika, and freshly ground black pepper to taste, and heat through. Stir in dry sherry. Transfer to a heated serving dish and serve immediately.

Serves 4

VARIATIONS

Creamed Turkey and Ham

Cook as in basic recipe (above) substituting 175 g/6 oz diced cooked ham for half the diced cooked turkey.

Creamed Turkey and Prawns

Cook as in basic recipe (above) substituting 175 g/6 oz peeled cooked prawns for half the diced cooked turkey.

Curried Creamed Turkey

Cook as in basic recipe (left) adding ½ to 1½ teaspoons curry powder and 50 g/2 oz freshly grated coconut with other seasonings.

Creamed Turkey with Black Olives

Cook as in basic recipe (left) using just 225 g/8 oz diced cooked turkey. Just before serving, add 4 chopped hard-boiled eggs and 75 g/3 oz thinly sliced stoned black olives.

Turkey Tetrazzini

450 g/1 lb cooked turkey, cut into thin
  slivers
225 g/8 oz spaghetti
salt and freshly ground black pepper
75 g/3 oz butter
100 g/4 oz button mushrooms, sliced
3 tablespoons flour
450 ml/¾ pint chicken stock
150 ml/¼ pint double cream
2 tablespoons dry sherry
4 tablespoons freshly grated Parmesan
  cheese

1.   Preheat oven to moderate (180 C, 350 F, gas 4).

2.   Cook spaghetti in 2 to 2.25 litres/3 to 4 pints boiling salted water for 12 to 15 minutes, or until spaghetti is tender but still *al dente*. Drain.

3.   Meanwhile, melt 40 g/1½ oz butter in a thick-bottomed frying pan and sauté sliced button mushrooms until golden brown.

4.   Melt remaining butter in a thick-bottomed saucepan, add flour and cook for 2 to 3 minutes, stirring constantly, until flour is cooked through. Gradually add chicken stock

and cook, stirring vigorously, until thick and smooth. Add double cream and dry sherry, season to taste with salt and freshly ground black pepper and heat through.

5.   Add mushrooms and turkey slivers to half the sauce. Add spaghetti to the other half. Arrange spaghetti round the edges of an ovenproof gratin dish. Pour turkey and mushroom mixture into the centre, sprinkle with freshly grated Parmesan cheese and bake in preheated oven until golden brown. Serve immediately, from the gratin dish.

Serves 4

Ham and Sweet Corn au Gratin

450 g/1 lb cooked ham, in one piece, diced
1 (340-g/12-oz) can sweet corn, drained
2 tablespoons finely chopped onion
1 small green pepper, deseeded and finely chopped.
350 ml/12 fl oz Quick White Sauce (page 49)
½ teaspoon mustard powder
4 tablespoons freshly grated Gruyère cheese
4 tablespoons fresh breadcrumbs
paprika

1.   Preheat oven to moderately hot (190 C, 375 F, gas 5).

2.   Place diced ham, sweet corn, finely chopped onion and green pepper in layers in an ovenproof gratin dish.

3.   Bring Quick White Sauce just to the boil. Add mustard powder and pour over ham and sweet corn mixture.

4.   Combine grated cheese and breadcrumbs and sprinkle over the sauce. Sprinkle with paprika and bake in preheated oven for 15 to 20 minutes, or until golden brown. Serve immediately, from the gratin dish.

Serves 6

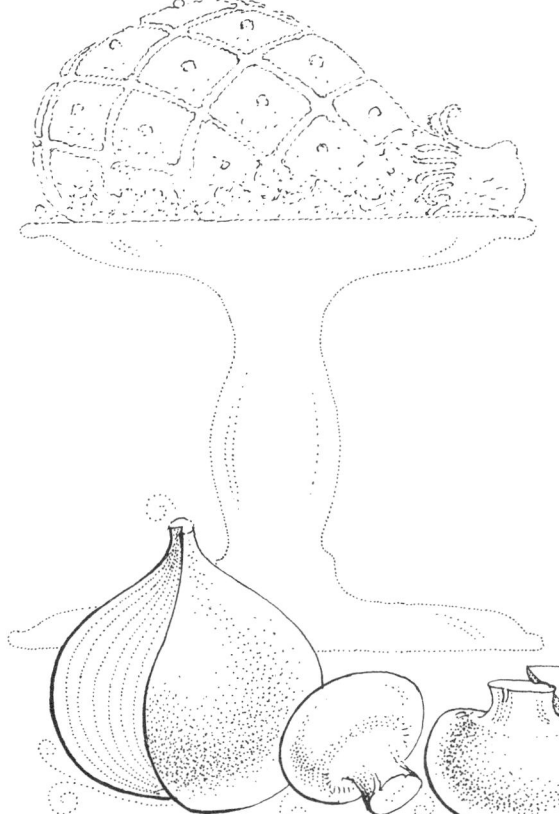

Jambon à la Crème aux Oranges

2 oranges
15 g/½ oz butter
1 tablespoon flour
150 ml/¼ pint port
salt and freshly ground black pepper
4 thick slices ham
1 egg yolk
150 ml/¼ pint double cream
sprigs of watercress

1.   Preheat oven to cool (140 C, 275 F, gas 1).

2.   Peel oranges and cut away all white pith. Slip knife blade between each segment and membrane and cut segment out. Remove any pips.

3.   Melt butter in a thick-bottomed saucepan, add flour and cook for 2 to 3 minutes, stirring constantly, until flour is cooked through. Gradually add port and cook, stirring vigorously, until thick and smooth. Season to taste with salt and freshly ground black pepper. Allow to cool.

4.   Meanwhile, place ham slices in an oven-proof gratin dish and heat through in pre-heated oven.

5.   When sauce is just warm, stir in egg yolk and double cream. Heat through; do not allow sauce to come to the boil. Pour over ham slices, garnish with orange segments and watercress sprigs and serve immediately, from the gratin dish.

Serves 4

Creamed Ham

350 g/12 oz cooked ham, in one piece, diced
450 ml/¾ pint Quick White Sauce (page 49)
¼ teaspoon mustard powder
few drops Tabasco sauce

1.   Combine diced ham and Quick White Sauce in a thick-bottomed saucepan and bring just to the boil.

2.   Add mustard powder and a few drops of Tabasco. Transfer to a heated serving dish and serve immediately.

Serves 6

VARIATIONS

Ham à la King

Cook as in basic recipe (above) adding 1 finely chopped canned pimiento, 3 tablespoons finely chopped green pepper and, if desired, 225 g/8 oz sliced button mushrooms which you have sautéed in butter.

Ham with Cheese Sauce

Cook as in basic recipe (above) substituting Mornay Sauce (page 52) for Quick White Sauce.

OTHER VARIATIONS

Cook as in basic recipe (above) adding any one of the following: 175 g/6 oz sweet corn, 75 g/3 oz cooked peas, 1 tablespoon chopped stoned black olives, or 3 tablespoons chili sauce.

Chili con Carne with Beans

65 g/2½ oz butter
1 tablespoon olive oil
575 g/1¼ lb lean sirloin or rump steak, minced
salt and freshly ground black pepper
2 Spanish onions, finely chopped
2 cloves garlic, finely chopped
2 tablespoons flour
3–4 tablespoons Mexican chili powder (see note below)
1 (150-g/5-oz) can tomato purée
3 tablespoons red wine vinegar
750 ml/1¼ pints beef stock
1 (425-g/15-oz) can pinto beans, drained

1.   Melt 15 g/½ oz butter with olive oil in a thick-bottomed casserole. Brown minced sirloin or rump steak, turning frequently to keep from sticking. Season to taste with salt and freshly ground black pepper.

2.   Melt remaining butter in a thick-bottomed saucepan and sauté finely chopped onion and garlic until onion begins to take on colour. Add flour and chili powder and cook for 2 to 3 minutes, stirring constantly, until flour is cooked through. Gradually add tomato purée, red wine vinegar and beef stock, and cook, stirring vigorously, until thick and smooth.

3.   Add sauce to casserole, cover and simmer for 20 minutes, or until beef is tender. Add pinto beans and heat through. Serve immediately, from the casserole.

Serves 6

Note   Be sure to use Mexican chili powder (a blend of spices) and not powdered chillies, which would make the dish inedibly hot.

Curried Chicken Hawaiian

1 (1.5 to 1.75-kg/3 to 4-lb) chicken
salt and freshly ground black pepper
3 tablespoons olive oil
1 large clove garlic, crushed
8 spring onions, cut into 2.5-cm/1-in pieces
450 ml/¾ pint chicken stock
300 ml/½ pint single cream
2 tablespoons flour
2 tablespoons curry powder
⅛ teaspoon ground turmeric
¼ teaspoon ground coriander
⅛ teaspoon cayenne
pinch of ground cinnamon
40 g/1½ oz sultanas, blanched
juice of 1 lime or lemon

1.   Cut chicken into pieces and season to taste.

2.   Heat olive oil in a thick-bottomed casserole. Sauté garlic until well browned. Discard.

3.   Add chicken pieces to casserole and sauté until golden brown on all sides.

4.   Pour off any fats remaining in casserole. Add spring onion pieces and stock, cover and simmer for 15 to 20 minutes, or until chicken pieces are tender.

5.   Combine single cream, flour, curry powder, ground turmeric, ground coriander, cayenne and ground cinnamon. Add to casserole and cook for a further 2 to 3 minutes, stirring constantly, until flour and spices are cooked through.

6.   Add sultanas and lime or lemon juice and serve immediately, from the casserole.

Serves 4 to 6

Green Pasta Shells with Sausage and Courgettes

225 g/8 oz cooked green pasta shells
225 g/8 oz mortadella, in one piece, diced
2 medium-sized courgettes, thinly sliced
butter
2 tablespoons olive oil
225 g/8 oz lean sirloin or rump steak, minced
salt and freshly ground black pepper
cayenne
2 (397-g/14-oz) cans tomato sauce, or an equal quantity of Instant Tomato Sauce (page 54)
$\frac{1}{2}$–1 teaspoon dried oregano
2 tablespoons finely chopped parsley

1. Preheat oven to moderate (180 C, 350 F, gas 4).

2. Place cooked pasta shells in a buttered ovenproof gratin dish.

3. Heat olive oil in a thick-bottomed frying pan and sauté diced mortadella and minced beef until just golden brown. Season to taste with salt and freshly ground black pepper. Transfer with a slotted spoon to gratin dish.

4. Sauté thinly sliced courgettes in fat remaining in pan until just tender. Season to taste with salt, freshly ground black pepper and cayenne. Add to gratin dish.

5. Combine tomato sauce, dried oregano and finely chopped parsley. Pour into gratin dish. Mix lightly and bake in preheated oven until heated through. Serve immediately, from the gratin dish.

Serves 4 to 6

Pot-au-Feu de Poissons

675 g/1$\frac{1}{2}$ lb turbot fillets, cut into bite-sized pieces, bones and trimmings reserved
675 g/1$\frac{1}{2}$ lb sole fillets, cut into bite-sized pieces, bones and trimmings reserved
3 shelled scallops
100 g/4 oz cooked prawns, peeled
4 sticks celery, cut into 5-cm/2-in pieces
2 carrots, cut into 5-cm/2-in pieces
4 leeks, cut into 5-cm/2-in pieces
50 g/2 oz butter
600 ml/1 pint chicken stock
salt and freshly ground black pepper
2 tablespoons flour
350 ml/12 fl oz double cream
cayenne
finely chopped parsley and chives

1. Cut celery, carrot and leek pieces into matchstick-sized strips.

2. Melt 25 g/1 oz butter in a thick-bottomed casserole and sauté celery, carrot and leek strips until celery is soft but not coloured. Add 300 ml/$\frac{1}{2}$ pint chicken stock and simmer until vegetables are just tender. Season to taste with salt and freshly ground black pepper. Remove vegetables from casserole with a slotted spoon. Keep warm.

3. Add remaining stock to casserole together with reserved turbot and sole bones and trimmings. Season generously with salt and freshly ground black pepper and bring to the boil. Remove fish bones and trimmings from casserole with a slotted spoon and discard. Reduce heat and skim surface of stock with a slotted spoon.

4. Poach turbot and sole pieces in hot stock for 5 to 7 minutes, or until the fish flakes easily

with a fork. Remove from casserole with a slotted spoon and keep warm.

5.   Poach scallops and peeled prawns in hot stock for 3 to 5 minutes, or until scallops are tender. Remove from casserole with a slotted spoon and keep warm.

6.   Cook hot stock over a high heat until it has reduced to one-third of its original quantity.

7.   Meanwhile, melt remaining butter in a thick-bottomed saucepan, add flour and cook for 2 to 3 minutes, stirring constantly, until flour is cooked through. Gradually add reduced fish stock and cook, stirring vigorously, until thick and smooth. Add double cream and a pinch of cayenne and heat through.

8.   To assemble the pot-au-feu, divide seafood between four to six individual heated serving bowls. Arrange vegetables among seafood and top with sauce. Sprinkle each bowl with finely chopped parsley and chives, and a little cayenne if desired, and serve immediately.

Serves 4 to 6

Chicken and Tuna Casserole with Sweet Corn

225 g/8 oz cooked chicken, diced
1 (198-g/7-oz) can tuna fish, drained and flaked
1 (198-g/7-oz) can sweet corn, drained
50 g/2 oz butter
4 tablespoons chopped onion
3 tablespoons chopped green pepper
2 tablespoons flour
350 ml/12 fl oz milk
1 teaspoon paprika
salt and freshly ground black pepper
6 tablespoons fresh breadcrumbs

1.   Preheat oven to moderate (160 C, 325 F, gas 3).

2.   Melt 25 g/1 oz butter in a thick-bottomed frying pan and sauté chopped onion and pepper until vegetables are soft but not coloured. Add flour and cook for 2 to 3 minutes, stirring constantly, until flour is cooked through. Gradually add milk and cook, stirring vigorously, until thick and smooth.

3.   Combine diced chicken, flaked tuna fish, sweet corn and sauce, and season to taste with paprika and salt and freshly ground black pepper. Pour into an ovenproof casserole, cover and bake in preheated oven until heated through.

4.   Meanwhile, melt remaining butter in a thick-bottomed frying pan and toss breadcrumbs in butter until golden brown. Sprinkle over chicken mixture and serve immediately, from the casserole.

Serves 4

Quails with White Grapes

4 oven-ready quails
75 g/3 oz seedless white grapes
2 tablespoons flour
salt and freshly ground white pepper
90 g/3½ oz butter
150 ml/¼ pint dry white wine
2 tablespoons lemon juice
4 slices white bread

1. Season flour generously with salt and freshly ground white pepper.

2. Rub seasoned flour into quails.

3. Melt 50 g/2 oz butter in a thick-bottomed casserole and sauté quails until golden brown on all sides. Add dry white wine and lemon juice. Lower heat, cover and simmer for 10 to 15 minutes.

4. Meanwhile, melt remaining butter in a thick-bottomed frying pan and sauté bread slices until golden brown on both sides. Drain on absorbent kitchen paper and keep warm.

5. Add seedless white grapes to casserole and continue to cook for a further 5 to 10 minutes, or until quails are tender. Serve each quail on a slice of fried bread, with the grapes and casserole juices spooned over.

Serves 4

Salmis of Partridge

3 cooked partridges
3 tablespoons mousse de foie gras
1–2 tablespoons Dijon mustard
6 tablespoons red wine or dry white wine
6 tablespoons beef stock
juice of 1–2 lemons
finely grated rind of 1 lemon
salt and freshly ground black pepper
freshly grated nutmeg
75 g/3 oz button mushrooms, sliced
beurre manié (made by mashing together
  1 teaspoon each of flour and butter to
  form a smooth paste)
finely chopped parsley

1. Cut partridges into serving pieces and place in a thick-bottomed casserole.

2. Mash *mousse de foie gras* with Dijon mustard. Add red wine or dry white wine, beef stock, lemon juice and finely grated lemon rind, and season to taste with salt, freshly ground black pepper and freshly grated nutmeg.

3. Add sliced mushrooms to sauce and pour into casserole. Cook until heated through, stirring occasionally so that each piece of bird is thoroughly moistened. Do not allow to come to the boil.

4. Add *beurre manié* to casserole, stirring constantly until butter has melted. Sprinkle with finely chopped parsley and serve immediately, from the casserole.

Serves 6

Quails with White Grapes

CHAPTER TEN

GREAT VEGETABLES

American Steamed Corn on the Cob

8 corn cobs
salt and freshly ground black pepper
cayenne
butter

1. Strip away husks and silk from corn cobs. Wash husks but do not dry them; the clinging drops of water make the steam. Line a thick-bottomed saucepan with husks.

2. Place corn cobs on husks, cover and steam for 20 to 25 minutes, or until tender. Transfer to a heated serving dish and serve immediately, with salt, freshly ground black pepper, cayenne and lashings of butter.

Serves 4

Grilled Corn on the Cob with Bacon

4 corn cobs
4 rashers green bacon
50 g/2 oz softened butter
salt and freshly ground black pepper
cayenne

1. Preheat grill to high.

2. Strip away husks and silk from corn cobs.

Spread each cob with softened butter and season to taste with salt, freshly ground black pepper and a little cayenne. Wrap 1 bacon rasher round each cob.

3. Wrap cobs tightly in foil and grill under preheated grill for 15 to 20 minutes, or until tender, turning frequently. Transfer to a heated serving dish. Open foil, roll back and serve immediately.

Serves 4

Picnic Succotash

225 g/8 oz button onions
salt and freshly ground black pepper
225 g/8 oz back bacon, in one piece, chopped
1 (283-g/10-oz) can green lima beans, drained
1 (340-g/12-oz) can sweet corn

1. Cook button onions in boiling salted water for 10 minutes, or until tender. Drain.

2. Meanwhile, sauté chopped bacon in a thick-bottomed frying pan until crisp. Remove from pan with a slotted spoon. Drain on absorbent kitchen paper.

3. Pour off all but 4 tablespoons bacon fat from pan and sauté onions until golden brown.

4. Return bacon to pan. Add lima beans and

sweet corn, together with sweet corn juices, and heat through. Season to taste with salt and freshly ground black pepper. Transfer to a heated serving dish and serve immediately.

Serves 4 to 6

Tomatoes and Onion in Foil

4 medium-sized firm tomatoes
4 paper-thin slices onion, cut to the size of tomatoes
salt and freshly ground black pepper
finely chopped basil or parsley
caster sugar

1. Preheat oven to moderately hot (190 C, 375 F, gas 5).

2. Cut tomatoes in half crossways. Season cut surfaces to taste with salt and freshly ground black pepper. Lay 1 onion slice on each of four cut tomato surfaces and sprinkle with finely chopped basil or parsley, and caster sugar. Re-form tomatoes and secure with wooden cocktail sticks.

3. Wrap each tomato in foil and bake in preheated oven for 15 to 20 minutes, or until tender. Remove foil and cocktail sticks, transfer to a heated serving dish and serve immediately.

Serves 4

Savoury Vegetables

16 cauliflower florets
16 broccoli florets
16 mange-tout peas
100 g/4 oz frozen peas
salt and freshly ground black pepper
50 g/2 oz butter
$\frac{1}{4}$ chicken stock cube, crumbled

1. Cook vegetables in separate pans of boiling salted water for 3 to 5 minutes, or until just tender. Drain and refresh under cold running water. Drain again.

2. Melt butter with crumbled $\frac{1}{4}$ stock cube in a thick-bottomed frying pan. Toss vegetables in butter until heated through. Season to taste with freshly ground black pepper. Transfer to a heated serving dish and serve immediately.

Serves 4

Peas au Beurre

450 g/1 lb frozen peas
50 g/2 oz butter
4 tablespoons chicken stock
salt and freshly ground black pepper
lemon juice

1. Place peas in a thick-bottomed saucepan. Pour in just enough cold water to cover and bring to the boil. Drain.

2. Return peas to pan together with butter and chicken stock. Season with salt and freshly ground black pepper and simmer, half-covered, for 10 minutes, or until liquid is almost absorbed and peas are tender, shaking pan occasionally. Transfer to a heated serving dish, sprinkle with lemon juice and serve.

Serves 4

Peas à la Française

675 g/1½ lb frozen peas
12 button onions
1 rasher bacon, 5 mm/¼ in thick
1 tablespoon olive oil
50 g/2 oz butter
4 tablespoons chicken stock
sugar
salt
lettuce leaves

1. Place peas in a thick-bottomed saucepan. Pour in just enough cold water to cover and bring to the boil. Drain.

2. Place button onions in another pan. Pour in just enough cold water to cover and bring to the boil. Drain.

3. Cut rind off bacon if necessary, then cut bacon into fingers 5 mm/¼ in wide. Heat olive oil in a thick-bottomed frying pan and sauté bacon fingers until golden brown. Drain on absorbent kitchen paper.

4. Combine peas, onions and bacon fingers in a thick-bottomed saucepan. Add butter and chicken stock and season to taste with sugar and salt. Cover and simmer for 10 minutes, or until liquid is almost absorbed and vegetables are tender; shake pan occasionally during cooking. Serve immediately, on a bed of lettuce leaves.

Serves 6

Purée Clamart

675 g/1½ lb frozen peas
75 g/3 oz butter
175 ml/6 fl oz chicken stock
1 medium-sized onion, finely chopped
salt and freshly ground black pepper
225 g/8 oz floury potatoes

1. Place peas in a thick-bottomed saucepan. Pour in just enough cold water to cover and bring to the boil. Drain.

2. Return peas to pan together with butter, chicken stock and finely chopped onion, and season to taste with salt and freshly ground black pepper. Cover and simmer for 10 minutes, or until liquid is almost absorbed and peas are tender; shake pan occasionally during cooking.

3. Meanwhile, cook potatoes in boiling salted water for 15 to 20 minutes, or until tender. Drain. Return to pan and toss over heat to evaporate any remaining moisture. Press through a fine sieve.

4. Place peas, together with cooking liquids, in the bowl of an electric blender or food processor and blend until smooth; do not pass through a sieve.

5. Gradually add pea purée to half the potato purée, stirring vigorously. If purée does not hold its shape, beat in a little more potato; the amount of potato purée used depends entirely on moisture of pea purée. Correct seasoning and transfer to a heated serving dish. Place dish over a saucepan of hot but not boiling water and heat through. Serve immediately.

Serves 6

Beets à l'Orange

1 (450-g/1-lb) jar small whole beetroot,
 drained and thinly sliced, 4 tablespoons
 juice reserved
1 teaspoon cornflour
2 tablespoons sugar
½ teaspoon salt
freshly ground black pepper
2 tablespoons lemon juice
4 tablespoons orange juice
finely grated rind of 1 orange
25 g/1 oz butter

1. Combine cornflour and sugar in a thick-bottomed saucepan and season with salt, and freshly ground black pepper to taste. Stir in lemon and orange juice and reserved beetroot juice.

2. Add finely grated orange rind to pan and cook, stirring vigorously, until sauce is thick and smooth and cornflour is cooked through.

3. Add thinly sliced beetroot to pan and heat through. Add butter, stirring constantly until butter has melted. Transfer to a heated serving dish and serve immediately.

Serves 4

French Beans en Persillade

675 g/1½ lb French beans
salt and freshly ground black pepper
50 g/2 oz softened butter
3 tablespoons finely chopped parsley

1. Cook French beans in boiling salted water for 5 minutes, or until just tender. Drain and refresh under cold running water. Drain again.

2. Combine softened butter and finely chopped parsley and season to taste with salt and freshly ground black pepper.

3. Melt herb butter in a thick-bottomed frying pan and toss beans in butter until heated through. Transfer to a heated serving dish, pour over buttery juices and serve immediately.

Serves 4 to 6

French Beans Amandine

675 g/1½ lb French beans
salt and freshly ground black pepper
65 g/2½ oz butter
75 g/3 oz blanched almonds, shredded
 and toasted
6 tablespoons finely chopped parsley

1. Cook French beans in boiling salted water for 5 minutes, or until just tender. Drain and refresh under cold running water. Drain again.

2. Melt butter in a thick-bottomed saucepan. Add shredded and toasted almonds and finely chopped parsley, and season to taste with salt and freshly ground black pepper. Toss beans in buttery juices until heated through. Transfer to a heated serving dish and serve immediately.

Serves 4 to 6

Vegetable Primavera

1 (227-g/8-oz) packet frozen broccoli
  florets, defrosted
1 (227-g/8-oz) packet frozen cauliflower
  florets, defrosted
225 g/8 oz French beans
3 sticks celery, halved lengthways and
  cut into 13-cm/5-in pieces
100 g/4 oz frozen peas
salt and freshly ground black pepper
1 (241-g/8½-oz) can asparagus spears
1 cucumber, cut into 5-mm/¼-in slices
hot chicken stock
225 g/8 oz courgettes
25 g/1 oz butter
3 tablespoons mixed finely chopped
  parsley, chives and chervil
lemon juice (optional)

1. Cook broccoli and cauliflower florets,
French beans, celery and peas in separate thick-
bottomed saucepans of boiling salted water for
3 to 5 minutes, or until just tender. Drain and
refresh under cold running water. Drain again.

2. At the same time, place asparagus spears,
with their can juices, in a pan and heat through.
Drain and refresh under cold running water.
Drain again. Place cucumber slices in another
pan, pour in just enough hot chicken stock to
cover and cook for 3 to 5 minutes, or until just
tender. Drain.

3. Score courgettes lengthways with a canelle
knife so that you have alternating bands of
green and white. Slice into thin rounds.

4. Melt butter in a thick-bottomed frying pan
and sauté courgette rounds until tender but still
crisp.

5. Add parboiled vegetables to pan and toss
until heated through. Season to taste with salt
and freshly ground black pepper.

6. Add finely chopped parsley, chives and
chervil to pan and toss again. Correct seasoning, adding a little lemon juice if desired.
Transfer to a heated serving dish and serve
immediately.

Serves 4 to 6

French Beans with Mushrooms

225 g/8 oz cooked French beans
100 g/4 oz button mushrooms, thinly
  sliced
25 g/1 oz butter
1 tablespoon olive oil
2 tablespoons finely chopped onion
lemon juice
salt and freshly ground black pepper
1 tablespoon finely chopped parsley

1. Melt butter with olive oil in a thick-
bottomed frying pan and sauté finely chopped
onion until soft but not coloured. Add thinly
sliced mushrooms and continue to sauté until
mushrooms are tender.

2. Add cooked French beans to pan and heat
through. Sprinkle with lemon juice and season
to taste with salt and freshly ground black
pepper. Transfer to a heated serving dish,
sprinkle with finely chopped parsley and serve
immediately.

Serves 4

Vegetable Primavera

Baked Potato Cake

450 g/1 lb potatoes, prebaked in their
  jackets
pinch of cayenne
salt and freshly ground black pepper
25 g/1 oz butter
1 tablespoon olive oil
4 tablespoons freshly grated Gruyère
  cheese

1.   Peel and coarsely grate prebaked potatoes.
Add a pinch of cayenne and season generously
with salt and freshly ground black pepper.
Divide into two equal portions.

2.   Melt butter with olive oil in a thick-
bottomed frying pan. Place one potato portion
in pan and pat into a round flat shape. Sauté
until underside is golden brown.

3.   Sprinkle surface of potato cake with
freshly grated Gruyère cheese. Place second
potato portion on top of first and pat into
shape. Turn potato cake over and sauté until
underside is golden brown, adding more oil if
necessary. Turn out on to a heated serving
platter and serve immediately.

Serves 4

Stuffed Baked Potatoes

6 medium-sized potatoes, prebaked in
  their jackets
4 tablespoons single cream
50 g/2 oz softened butter
4–6 tablespoons freshly grated Parmesan
  cheese
salt and freshly ground black pepper
freshly grated nutmeg
cayenne

1.   Preheat oven to moderately hot (190 C,
375 C, gas 5).

2.   Cut a thin slice from the top of each potato
and scoop out pulp, leaving a firm shell.

3.   Mash together potato pulp, single cream,
butter and freshly grated Parmesan cheese.
Season to taste with salt, freshly ground black
pepper, freshly grated nutmeg and cayenne.
Pile mashed potato back into shells and bake in
preheated oven until heated through. Transfer
to a heated serving dish and serve immediately.

Serves 6

Baked Potato Loaves

675 g/1½ lb potatoes, preboiled in their
  jackets
50 g/2 oz softened butter
3 tablespoons freshly grated Parmesan
  cheese
salt and freshly ground black pepper
2 eggs, well beaten
1 tablespoon fresh breadcrumbs

1.   Preheat oven to hot (220 C, 425 F, gas 7).

2.   Peel potatoes and mash them with butter
and 2 tablespoons freshly grated Parmesan
cheese. Season to taste with salt and freshly
ground black pepper. Beat in 1 well-beaten
egg. Divide mixture into 12 equal portions.

3.   Roll each potato portion into a fat oval
shape and pat each oval into the shape of a small
loaf. Cut diagonal slashes across the top of each
loaf and brush tops with remaining well-beaten
egg.

4.   Combine remaining cheese and the breadcrumbs, and sprinkle over each loaf. Bake in

preheated oven for 15 to 20 minutes, or until puffed and golden brown. Transfer to a heated serving dish and serve immediately.

Serves 6

Pommes de Terre au Lard

6 medium-sized potatoes, prebaked in their jackets
6 rashers back bacon
butter
finely chopped parsley

1. Preheat oven to hot (230 C, 450 F, gas 8).

2. Preheat grill to high.

3. Wrap each potato in foil and re-bake in preheated oven until heated through.

4. Meanwhile, roll up bacon rashers and grill under preheated grill until crisp. Drain on absorbent kitchen paper.

5. Cut a thin slice from the top of each potato and scoop out pulp, leaving a firm shell.

6. Pass pulp through a potato ricer or fine sieve, then pile back into shells. Top each with a bacon roll. Dot with butter, sprinkle with finely chopped parsley and serve immediately.

Serves 6

French Fried Potatoes

1.5 kg/3 lb old potatoes
oil for deep frying
salt

1. Peel potatoes and cut into even-sized sticks measuring 6×1 cm/$2\frac{1}{2} \times \frac{1}{2}$ in. Wash under cold running water for 5 minutes to remove excess starch. Drain. Dry carefully.

2. Meanwhile, heat oil in a deep saucepan or deep-fryer to a temperature of 120 C, 250 F.

3. Fry potato sticks in hot oil, in small batches, until soft but not coloured. Drain on absorbent kitchen paper.

4. Increase oil temperature to 190 C, 375 F and fry potato sticks again, in small batches, until crisp and golden brown. Drain on absorbent kitchen paper. Transfer to a heated serving dish, sprinkle with salt and serve immediately.

Serves 6

VARIATIONS

Pommes Allumettes

Prepare, fry and serve potatoes as in basic recipe (above), but cut potatoes into matchstick-sized sticks.

Pommes Paille

Prepare, fry and serve potatoes as in basic recipe (above), but cut potatoes into fine *julienne* and fry only once, at 190 C, 375 F; stir for the first 20 seconds of frying.

Pommes Chips

Prepare, fry and serve potatoes as in basic recipe (above), but cut potatoes into thin rounds and fry only once, at 190 C, 375 F.

Pommes Anna

800 g/1¾ lb even-sized floury potatoes
100 g/4 oz butter, melted
salt and freshly ground black pepper
coarsely chopped parsley

1. Preheat oven to very hot (240 C, 475 F, gas 9).

2. Peel potatoes into even-sized barrel shapes and slice very thinly.

3. Heat 1 tablespoon butter in a flameproof round dish. When butter is sizzling, lower heat and cover base of dish with overlapping potato slices, arranged in a spiral. Season to taste with salt and freshly ground black pepper. Repeat until all potato slices are used, pouring over 1 tablespoon butter and seasoning between each layer. Finish by pouring over remaining butter.

4. Remove dish from heat, press potato slices well down in dish and bake in preheated oven for 20 minutes, or until tender. Drain off any excess butter. Turn potatoes out on to a heated serving platter, sprinkle with coarsely chopped parsley and serve immediately.

Serves 4

Pommes Annette

800 g/1¾ lb floury potatoes
40 g/1½ oz butter
salt and freshly ground black pepper

1. Preheat oven to moderately hot (200 C, 400 F, gas 6).

2. Peel potatoes, slice thinly and then cut into fine, even-sized strips.

3. Melt butter in a thick-bottomed frying pan and toss potato strips in butter until they just begin to take on colour. Season to taste with salt and freshly ground black pepper.

4. Butter an ovenproof round dish. Place potato strips in dish, press them down, bringing the edges in slightly, and bake in preheated oven for 10 minutes. Turn and continue to cook for a further 10 minutes, or until tender. Turn out on to a heated serving platter and serve immediately.

Serves 4

Mashed Sweet Potatoes

6 medium-sized sweet potatoes, prebaked
  in their jackets
50 g/2 oz softened butter
salt and freshly ground black pepper
150 ml/¼ pint hot milk

1. Peel prebaked potatoes, and mash with softened butter. Season to taste with salt and freshly ground black pepper.

2. Gradually beat in hot milk and continue to beat until potatoes are fluffy and smooth. Transfer to a heated serving dish and serve immediately.

Serves 6

Pommes Anna (top) and Pommes Annette (bottom)

Stir-Braised Carrots and Celery

225 g/8 oz carrots, thinly sliced
1 small head celery, cut into 2-cm/¾-in dice
4 tablespoons olive oil
1 clove garlic, finely chopped
6 tablespoons chicken stock
2 teaspoons soy sauce

1. Heat olive oil in a thick-bottomed frying pan. Add finely chopped garlic and, when garlic begins to sizzle, add thinly sliced carrots and diced celery. Sauté until celery is soft but not coloured.

2. Pour chicken stock into pan and bring to the boil. Stir in soy sauce.

3. Reduce heat, cover and cook for 10 minutes, or until vegetables are just tender and liquid in pan is reduced to 2 or 3 tablespoons. Transfer to a heated serving dish and serve immediately.

Serves 4

Batonnets of Carrots and Turnips

225 g/8 oz carrots
225 g/8 oz turnips
salt
40 g/1½ oz butter
1 tablespoon olive oil
finely chopped parsley

ROBERT CARRIER'S DRY MARINADE
½ chicken stock cube
4 tablespoons lemon juice
pinch of cayenne

1. Cut carrots and turnips into even-sized sticks measuring 5.5 cm × 5 mm/2¼ × ¼ in.

2. Cook carrot and turnip sticks in separate saucepans of lightly salted boiling water for 2 to 3 minutes, or until just tender. Drain and refresh under cold running water. Drain again.

3. Combine ingredients for dry marinade in an earthenware or porcelain (not metal) bowl.

4. Toss vegetables in dry marinade and allow to stand for 5 to 10 minutes, to absorb flavours.

5. Melt butter with olive oil in a thick-bottomed frying pan and sauté vegetables until tender but still crisp. Transfer to a heated serving dish, sprinkle with finely chopped parsley and serve immediately.

Serves 4

Batonnets of Potatoes, Turnips, Carrots and Cucumber

100 g/4 oz potatoes
100 g/4 oz turnips
100 g/4 oz carrots
½ small cucumber
salt
40 g/1½ oz butter
1 tablespoon olive oil
finely chopped parsley

ROBERT CARRIER'S DRY MARINADE
½ chicken stock cube
4 tablespoons lemon juice
pinch of cayenne

1. Cut potatoes, turnips, carrots and cucumber into even-sized sticks measuring 5.5 cm × 5 mm/2¼ × ¼ in.

2. Cook potato sticks in lightly salted boiling water for 3 to 4 minutes or until just tender. Drain and refresh under cold running water. Drain again.

3. At the same time, cook turnip, carrot and cucumber sticks in separate saucepans of lightly salted boiling water for 2 to 3 minutes, or until just tender. Drain and refresh under cold running water. Drain again.

4. Combine ingredients for dry marinade in an earthenware or porcelain (not metal) bowl.

5. Toss vegetables in dry marinade and allow to stand for 5 to 10 minutes, to absorb flavours.

6. Melt butter with olive oil in a thick-bottomed frying pan and sauté vegetables until tender but still crisp. Transfer to a heated serving dish, sprinkle with finely chopped parsley and serve immediately.

Serves 4

Crisp-Fried Courgettes

6 medium-sized courgettes
50 g/2 oz butter
salt and freshly ground black pepper
finely chopped parsley, chives and
** chervil**

1. Score courgettes lengthways with a canelle knife so that you have alternating bands of green and white. Slice into thin rounds.

2. Melt butter in a thick-bottomed frying pan and toss courgette rounds in butter until tender but still crisp. Season to taste with salt and freshly ground black pepper. Transfer to a heated serving dish, sprinkle with finely chopped parsley, chives and chervil and serve immediately.

Serves 4

Julienne of Courgettes with Spring Onions

6 medium-sized courgettes
4 spring onions, finely chopped
50 g/2 oz butter
salt and freshly ground black pepper

1. Cut courgettes into even-sized lengths and then into fine *julienne*.

2. Melt butter in a thick-bottomed frying pan and toss courgette strips in butter for 1 minute. Add finely chopped spring onions and continue to toss until vegetables are tender but still crisp. Season to taste with salt and freshly ground black pepper. Transfer to a heated serving dish and serve immediately.

Serves 4

Courgettes with Walnuts

6 medium-sized courgettes
12 walnut halves, coarsely chopped
50 g/2 oz butter
1 tablespoon finely chopped onion
2 teaspoons lemon juice
salt and freshly ground black pepper
finely chopped parsley

1. Score courgettes lengthways with a canelle knife to give alternating bands of green and white. Cut into thin rounds.

2. Melt butter in a frying pan and toss courgette rounds and finely chopped onion in the butter until vegetables are tender but still crisp.

3. Add walnut halves and lemon juice to pan, season to taste with salt and freshly ground black pepper and heat through. Transfer to a heated serving dish, sprinkle with parsley and serve immediately.

Serves 4

Stuffed Spanish Onions

(A wonderful way with leftovers)

4 cooked Spanish onions
2 slices white bread
225 g/8 oz cooked veal or chicken, chopped
100 g/4 oz cooked spinach, chopped
4 tablespoons chopped parsley
1 egg yolk
salt and freshly ground black pepper
6 tablespoons fresh breadcrumbs
4 tablespoons melted butter
1 tablespoon olive oil

1. Preheat oven to moderately hot (190 C, 375 F, gas 5).

2. Cut onions in half horizontally. Remove layers from centre of each $\frac{1}{2}$ onion, leaving a shell about 5 mm/$\frac{1}{4}$ in thick. Coarsely chop removed onion layers.

3. Soak bread slices in water. Squeeze until almost dry and shred coarsely.

4. Combine coarsely chopped onion and bread, chopped veal or chicken, spinach and parsley. Moisten mixture with egg yolk and season to taste with salt and freshly ground black pepper. Mound into onion shells, top with breadcrumbs and spoon over melted butter and olive oil. Bake in preheated oven for 15 to 20 minutes, or until breadcrumbs are golden brown. Transfer to a heated serving dish and serve immediately.

Serves 4

Stuffed Spanish Onions

Ginger Spinach with Soy

1.5 kg/3 lb fresh spinach
2 thin slices fresh root ginger, cut into
  thin strips
1–2 tablespoons soy sauce
3 tablespoons corn oil
salt and freshly ground black pepper

1.   Wash spinach leaves several times in cold water. Drain. Remove coarse stems and any damaged or yellowed leaves.

2.   Heat corn oil in a wok or thick-bottomed frying pan and sauté spinach and root ginger strips until ginger strips are soft but not coloured. Season to taste with salt and freshly ground black pepper.

3.   Pour off excess liquids from pan, add soy sauce and stir lightly. Transfer to a heated serving dish and serve immediately.

Serves 4 to 6

French Beans with Tomatoes

350 g/12 oz cooked French beans, cut into
  even-sized pieces
3 tomatoes, peeled, deseeded and diced
25 g/1 oz butter
1 tablespoon olive oil
2 tablespoons finely chopped onion
1 small clove garlic, finely chopped
lemon juice
salt and freshly ground black pepper
finely chopped parsley

1.   Melt butter with olive oil in a thick-bottomed frying pan and sauté finely chopped onion and garlic until soft but not coloured.

2.   Add cooked French bean pieces to pan and toss until heated through. Sprinkle with lemon juice and season to taste with salt and freshly ground black pepper.

3.   Add peeled, deseeded and diced tomatoes to pan and toss again to combine flavours and heat through. Transfer to a heated serving dish, sprinkle with finely chopped parsley and serve immediately.

Serves 4

Spring Onions Hollandaise

2 large or 4 small bunches spring onions
salt

HOLLANDAISE SAUCE
100 g/4 oz unsalted butter
lemon juice
pinch each of salt and freshly ground
  white pepper
4 egg yolks

1.   To make Hollandaise Sauce, divide butter into four even-sized pieces. Pour 1 teaspoon lemon juice and 1 tablespoon water into the top of a double saucepan and add a pinch each of salt and freshly ground white pepper. Add egg yolks and a quarter of the butter and stir vigorously and constantly over hot but not boiling water until butter has melted and sauce begins to thicken. Add second piece of butter and, as butter begins to melt, add third piece, stirring from the bottom of the pan until butter has melted. Add remaining piece of butter, stirring vigorously and constantly until butter has melted. Be careful not to allow water over which sauce is cooking to boil at any time.

Remove top part of pan from heat and continue to stir for 2 to 3 minutes. Set pan over water again and continue to stir for a further 2 minutes. By this time the emulsion should have formed and your sauce will be thick and creamy. 'Finish' sauce with a few drops of lemon juice. Strain through a fine sieve and keep warm.

2. Tie spring onions into four even-sized bunches and cook in boiling salted water for 6 to 8 minutes, or until bulbs are tender. Drain.

3. Untie spring onion bunches and transfer to a heated serving dish. Spoon over Hollandaise Sauce, leaving white bulbs and a little of the green tips free of sauce for colour and serve immediately.

Serves 4

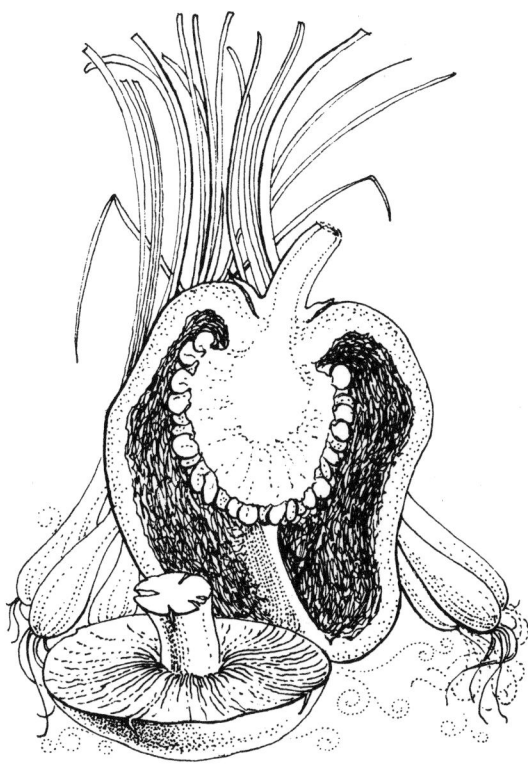

Anchoïade of Vegetables

8 large mushrooms, thickly sliced
4 tablespoons chopped chives or parsley
4 large tomatoes, thinly sliced
2 green peppers, deseeded and sliced crossways into rings
2 yellow peppers, deseeded and sliced lengthways
1 cucumber, peeled and sliced
2 bunches watercress, cut into sprigs

ANCHOÏADE SAUCE
150 ml/¼ pint olive oil
2–3 tablespoons red wine vinegar
2–3 cloves garlic, finely chopped
2–3 tablespoons finely chopped parsley
1 teaspoon Dijon mustard
6 anchovy fillets, chopped
freshly ground black pepper

1. To make Anchoïade Sauce, combine olive oil, red wine vinegar, finely chopped garlic and parsley. Combine Dijon mustard and chopped anchovy fillets in a mortar, pound to a smooth paste and stir into sauce. Season to taste with freshly ground black pepper.

2. Roll tops of thickly sliced mushrooms in chopped chives or parsley.

3. Arrange prepared vegetables and sprigs of watercress on a rectangular serving tray or wooden chopping board. Serve with Anchoïade Sauce handed separately. Guests help themselves to a selection of vegetables and spoon over a little sauce.

Serves 4

Aubergine Fritters

675 g/1½ lb small aubergines
3 tablespoons flour
salt and freshly ground black pepper
oil for deep drying

ROBERT CARRIER'S DRY MARINADE
½ chicken stock cube, crumbled
4 tablespoons lemon juice
pinch of cayenne

FRITTER BATTER
100 g/4 oz flour
pinch of salt
2 tablespoons olive oil
1 egg white
freshly ground black pepper

1. Combine ingredients for dry marinade in an earthenware or porcelain (not metal) bowl.

2. Slice aubergines into 5-mm/¼-in rings and then into even-sized strips 5 mm/¼ in thick. Toss in dry marinade and allow to stand for 5 to 10 minutes, to absorb flavours.

3. Meanwhile, prepare fritter batter. Sift together flour and salt and make a well in the centre. Pour in olive oil and 8 tablespoons lukewarm water and beat until smooth; the batter should be thicker than a crêpe batter. Whisk egg white until stiff but not dry and fold into batter. Season to taste with freshly ground black pepper.

4. Place flour in a shallow dish and season generously with salt and freshly ground black pepper.

5. Pat aubergine strips dry and toss in seasoned flour, shaking off excess.

6. Heat oil in a deep saucepan or deep-fryer to a temperature of 190 C, 375 F; a 2.5-cm/1-in

cube of day-old bread takes 1 minute to turn crisp and golden brown at this temperature.

7. Dip aubergine strips in batter, draining carefully, and deep fry in preheated oil for 2 to 3 minutes, or until crisp and golden brown. Drain on absorbent kitchen paper. Transfer to a heated serving dish and serve immediately.

Serves 4 to 6

Curried Cauliflower

1 (675-g/1½-lb) cauliflower, cut into florets
salt and freshly ground black pepper
25 g/1 oz butter
1 medium-sized onion, finely chopped
1½ teaspoons curry powder
3 tablespoons flour
2 tablespoons lemon juice
1 tablespoon tomato purée
450 ml/¾ pint milk
2 tablespoons finely chopped parsley
2 rashers bacon, grilled and finely chopped

1. Cook cauliflower florets in boiling salted water for 3 to 5 minutes, or until just tender. Drain and refresh under cold running water. Drain again.

2. Melt butter in a thick-bottomed frying pan and sauté finely chopped onion until soft but not coloured. Add curry powder and flour and cook for 2 to 3 minutes, stirring constantly, until flour is cooked through. Add lemon juice and tomato purée and season to taste with salt and freshly ground black pepper. Gradually add milk, stirring vigorously, and bring to the boil.

3. Add cauliflower florets to pan. Reduce heat and simmer until sauce is smooth and

creamy and just coats the florets. Transfer to a heated serving dish, sprinkle with finely chopped parsley and bacon and serve immediately.

Serves 6

Dutch Potato Purée with Apple and Bacon

1 kg/2 lb medium-sized potatoes, quartered
450 g/1 lb medium-sized dessert apples, peeled, cored and sliced
450 g/1 lb medium-sized cooking apples, peeled, cored and sliced
4–6 rashers smoked bacon
25 g/1 oz lard
100 g/4 oz butter, diced
salt and freshly ground black pepper

1.   Place potato quarters in a thick-bottomed saucepan and pour in enough water to cover. Bring to the boil, reduce heat and simmer for 10 minutes.

2.   Add sliced dessert and cooking apples to pan and continue to cook, stirring occasionally, for a further 5 minutes or until the potatoes and apples are tender.

3.   Meanwhile, melt lard in a thick-bottomed frying pan and fry bacon rashers until crisp. Drain on absorbent kitchen paper and chop coarsely.

4.   Drain potato quarters and apple slices and return to pan. Stir in diced butter and continue to cook, whisking constantly, until mixture has the consistency of a smooth purée; add a little

extra water or butter, if necessary. Season to taste with a little salt and freshly ground black pepper. Transfer to a heated serving dish, sprinkle with coarsely chopped bacon and serve immediately.

Serves 4 to 6

Broccoli Towers

2 (227-g/8-oz) packets frozen broccoli florets, defrosted
6 tablespoons milk
6 tablespoons double cream
2 eggs
salt and freshly ground black pepper

1.   Preheat oven to moderate (180 C, 350 F, gas 4).

2.   Trim stalks from broccoli and cook according to packet directions.

3.   Place broccoli, milk, double cream and eggs in the bowl of an electric blender or food processor. Season to taste with salt and freshly ground black pepper and blend to a smooth purée. Divide mixture between eight buttered (75-ml/3-fl oz) dariole moulds and cover with buttered foil. Stand moulds in a roasting tin and pour in enough hot water to come half-way up the sides of the moulds. Bake in preheated oven for 10 to 15 minutes, or until set.

4.   Run a knife round the edge of each mould. Turn towers out on to a heated serving platter and serve immediately.

Serves 8

CHAPTER ELEVEN

SUPER SALADS

Salade Niçoise

1 lettuce
4 tomatoes, quartered and deseeded
1 Spanish onion, sliced
1 red or green pepper, deseeded and sliced
2 sticks celery, sliced
100 g/4 oz cooked French beans
1 (198-g/7-oz) can tuna fish, drained (optional)
8–12 canned anchovy fillets (optional)
2 canned artichoke hearts, sliced (optional)
8 radishes, cut into flower shapes or sliced (optional)
black olives (optional)
2 or 3 hard-boiled eggs, quartered (optional)

DRESSING
6 tablespoons olive oil
2 tablespoons red wine vinegar
$\frac{1}{2}$ teaspoon Dijon mustard
1–2 cloves garlic, finely chopped
8–12 basil leaves, coarsely chopped
salt and freshly ground black pepper

1. Wash and prepare lettuce. Shake dry in a salad basket or dry each leaf carefully with absorbent kitchen paper.

2. Combine quartered tomatoes, sliced onion, red or green pepper and celery, and French beans.

3. To make the dressing, combine olive oil, red wine vinegar, Dijon mustard, finely chopped garlic and coarsely chopped basil. Season to taste with salt and freshly ground black pepper.

4. Pour dressing over vegetables and toss until all ingredients glisten.

5. Arrange lettuce leaves in the centre of a round serving platter or salad bowl. Pile vegetables on to leaves. Before serving, garnish with some or all of the following: tuna fish, anchovy fillets, sliced artichoke hearts, radish 'flowers' or slices, black olives and quartered hard-boiled eggs.

Serves 4 to 6

Salade Niçoise

Tossed Green Salad

1 or 2 lettuces

DRESSING
1 tablespoon lemon juice
2 tablespoons red wine vinegar
$\frac{1}{4}$–$\frac{1}{2}$ teaspoon Dijon mustard
salt and freshly ground black pepper
6–8 tablespoons olive oil
$\frac{1}{2}$ clove garlic, finely chopped
2 tablespoons finely chopped parsley, or a combination of chopped parsley and tarragon

1. Wash and prepare lettuce. Shake dry in a salad basket or dry each leaf carefully with absorbent kitchen paper.

2. To make the dressing, combine lemon juice, red wine vinegar and Dijon mustard and season to taste with salt and freshly ground black pepper. Add olive oil, beating with a fork until mixture emulsifies. Add finely chopped garlic, and parsley or parsley and tarragon.

3. To serve, pour the dressing into a salad bowl and arrange lettuce leaves in bowl. Toss at the table until each leaf glistens.

Serves 4 to 6

VARIATIONS

A Prepare salad as in basic recipe (above), augmenting lettuce with finely chopped raw courgettes and shredded Chinese cabbage leaves (bokchoy).

B Prepare salad as in basic recipe (above), augmenting lettuce with lightly cooked slivered mange-tout peas and French beans.

C Prepare salad as in basic recipe (above), adding finely chopped lemon grass to dressing.

D Prepare salad as in basic recipe (left), augmenting lettuce with curly endive and watercress sprigs.

Coleslaw with Green Pepper and Raisins

1 (450-g/1-lb) white cabbage, finely shredded
1 small green pepper, deseeded and chopped
50 g/2 oz raisins, blanched
175 g/6 oz back bacon, in one piece, chopped
4 tablespoons lemon juice
1 teaspoon salt
6 tablespoons mayonnaise
4 tablespoons chopped parsley
2 sticks celery, chopped
2 tablespoons finely chopped onion

1. Sauté chopped bacon in a thick-bottomed frying pan until crisp. Remove from pan with a slotted spoon, reserving dripping. Drain on absorbent kitchen paper.

2. Combine 4 tablespoons bacon dripping, lemon juice, salt and mayonnaise.

3. Combine bacon, finely shredded cabbage, chopped green pepper, blanched raisins, chopped parsley and celery and finely chopped onion in a salad bowl. Add mayonnaise and toss lightly until all ingredients are evenly coated. Chill before serving.

Serves 6

Raw Spinach Salad with Bacon and Beans

450 g/1 lb young spinach leaves
4 cooked rashers bacon, cut into even-
  sized squares
1 (170-g/6-oz) can lima beans or haricots
  blancs, drained
½ small onion, thinly sliced
salt and freshly ground black pepper
6–8 tablespoons olive oil
2 tablespoons red wine vinegar
½ teaspoon mustard powder
1 clove garlic, finely chopped
2 tablespoons finely chopped parsley

1. Wash spinach several times in cold water. Drain. Remove coarse stems and any yellowed or damaged leaves. Chill.

2. Soak thinly sliced onion in salted iced water for 10 minutes. Drain.

3. Meanwhile, combine olive oil and red wine vinegar (three to four parts olive oil to one part red wine vinegar). Add mustard powder, finely chopped garlic and parsley, and season to taste with salt and freshly ground black pepper.

4. Arrange spinach leaves in a salad bowl. Pour over dressing and toss until each leaf glistens. Garnish with thinly sliced onion, bacon squares and lima beans or haricots blancs and serve.

Serves 4 to 6

Mâche and Beetroot Salad

225 g/8 oz lamb's lettuce
1 (227-g/8-oz) jar diced beetroot, drained
6 tablespoons olive oil
2 tablespoons lemon juice
salt and freshly ground black pepper

1. Wash lamb's lettuce and remove stalks and any damaged leaves. Dry carefully with absorbent kitchen paper.

2. Rinse diced beetroot. Drain.

3. Combine olive oil and lemon juice in a salad bowl and season to taste with salt and freshly ground black pepper. Add lamb's lettuce and beetroot. Toss until all ingredients glisten and serve.

Serves 4

Beetroot and Cauliflower Salad Bowl

450 g/1 lb cooked beetroot, diced
1 small cauliflower
salt
1 medium-sized stick celery, chopped
1 tablespoon finely chopped spring
  onion
150 ml/¼ pint French Dressing (page 159)

1. Remove green leaves from cauliflower, trim stem and cut off any bruised spots. Break into florets.

2. Cook cauliflower florets in lightly salted boiling water for 4 to 5 minutes, or until just tender. Drain and refresh under cold running water. Drain again. Chill.

3. Combine chilled cauliflower florets, diced beetroot, chopped celery and finely chopped spring onion in a salad bowl. Pour over French Dressing. Toss until all ingredients glisten and serve.

Serves 4

Prawn and French Bean Salad

350 g/12 oz cooked prawns, peeled
350 g/12 oz French beans, cut into
  2.5-cm/1-in pieces
salt
1 radicchio
2 tablespoons coarsely chopped spring
  onion or shallot
sprigs of watercress (optional)

DRESSING
generous 150 ml/¼ pint olive oil
3 tablespoons red wine vinegar
2 tablespoons finely chopped parsley
1 clove garlic, finely chopped
salt and freshly ground black pepper

1. Cook French bean pieces in boiling salted water for 4 to 5 minutes, or until just tender. Drain and refresh under cold running water. Drain again.

2. Wash and prepare radicchio. Shake dry in a salad basket or dry each leaf carefully with absorbent kitchen paper.

3. To make the dressing, combine olive oil, red wine vinegar and finely chopped parsley and garlic, and season to taste with salt and freshly ground black pepper.

4. Combine beans, peeled prawns and coarsely chopped spring onion or shallot in a salad bowl or four individual bowls. Pour over dressing and toss until all ingredients glisten. Garnish with radicchio, and sprigs of watercress if desired, and serve.

Serves 4

Prawn and French Bean Salad

Potato Salad

1 kg/2 lb new potatoes, in their jackets
salt and freshly ground black pepper
6–8 tablespoons olive oil
6–8 tablespoons dry white wine or beef
  consommé
2 tablespoons red wine vinegar
4 tablespoons finely chopped shallot
2 tablespoons finely chopped parsley or
  dill

1. Cook potatoes in their jackets in boiling salted water for 15 to 20 minutes, or until tender. Drain.

2. Meanwhile, make a dressing by combining olive oil, dry white wine or beef consommé, and red wine vinegar (three to four parts olive oil and dry white wine or beef consommé to one part red wine vinegar). Add finely chopped shallot, and parsley or dill, and season to taste with salt and freshly ground black pepper.

3. Peel potatoes and slice thickly. Arrange in a salad bowl. While potatoes are still hot, pour over dressing. Toss lightly until each slice glistens and serve.

Serves 4 to 6

Potato Salad Niçoise

1 x recipe quantity Potato Salad (above)
2 (50-g/1¾-oz) cans anchovy fillets,
  drained
stoned black olives
4–6 small ripe tomatoes, thickly sliced
3–4 hard-boiled eggs, sliced

1. Arrange anchovy fillets in a square lattice on top of the potato salad and place a black olive in the centre of each square.

2. Garnish salad with a ring of tomato slices topped with egg slices.

Serves 4 to 6

Orange Rice Salad

225 g/8 oz cooked rice
4 tablespoons orange juice
4 teaspoons grated orange rind
7 tablespoons olive oil
2 sticks celery, finely chopped
4 tablespoons finely chopped onion
6 tablespoons hot chicken stock (made
  with $\frac{1}{4}$ chicken stock cube)
2 tablespoons lemon juice
pinch of cayenne
salt and freshly ground black pepper
lettuce leaves
3–4 tablespoons toasted slivered almonds

1. Heat 3 tablespoons olive oil in a thick-bottomed saucepan and sauté finely chopped celery and onion until vegetables are soft but not coloured. Set aside.

2. Combine hot chicken stock, orange juice, grated orange rind and lemon juice, and season with cayenne, and salt and freshly ground black pepper to taste.

3. Combine rice, prepared vegetables and orange-flavoured liquid in a thick-bottomed saucepan. Simmer for 1 to 2 minutes, or until all the liquid has been absorbed. Allow to cool, then chill.

4. Pour remaining olive oil over salad and toss until all ingredients glisten. Arrange on a bed of lettuce leaves, scatter with toasted slivered almonds and serve.

Serves 4

Green Rice Salad

450 g/1 lb cooked rice
175 g/6 oz spinach
8 cauliflower florets
225 g/8 oz French beans, cut into
 1-cm/$\frac{1}{2}$-in pieces
salt
1 tablespoon olive oil
2 medium-sized courgettes, thinly sliced
150 ml/$\frac{1}{4}$ pint French Dressing (page 159)
4 tablespoons cooked peas
2 tablespoons finely chopped parsley

1. Wash spinach several times in cold water. Drain. Remove coarse stems and any damaged or yellowed leaves.

2. Cook cauliflower florets, French bean pieces and spinach in separate thick-bottomed saucepans of boiling salted water for 3 to 5 minutes, or until just tender. Drain and refresh under cold running water. Drain again.

3. Press spinach between your hands to get rid of excess moisture. Chop finely.

4. Heat olive oil in a thick-bottomed frying pan and toss thinly sliced courgettes in oil for 1 to 2 minutes, or until just tender. Remove from pan with a slotted spoon. Allow to cool.

5. Combine spinach and French Dressing.

6. Place cooked rice in a salad bowl, add spinach dressing and toss until each grain of rice glistens. Add prepared vegetables, cooked peas and finely chopped parsley. Toss again until all ingredients glisten and serve.

Serves 6

Saffron Rice Salad

225 g/8 oz long-grain rice
$\frac{1}{4}$ teaspoon ground saffron
750 ml/1$\frac{1}{4}$ pints chicken stock
6 tablespoons dry white wine
salt and freshly ground black pepper
4 tomatoes, sliced
black olives

DRESSING
6–8 tablespoons olive oil
2 tablespoons red wine vinegar
4 tablespoons finely chopped parsley
1–2 cloves garlic, finely chopped
mustard powder
salt and freshly ground black pepper

1. Combine chicken stock, ground saffron and dry white wine in a thick-bottomed saucepan and bring to the boil. Add long-grain rice, season to taste with salt and freshly ground black pepper, and cook for 15 to 18 minutes, or until tender but not mushy. Drain and allow to cool.

2. To make the dressing, combine olive oil and red wine vinegar (three to four parts olive oil to one part red wine vinegar) with finely chopped parsley and garlic. Season to taste with mustard powder, salt and freshly ground black pepper.

3. Toss rice in dressing until each grain glistens. Transfer to a serving platter, garnish with sliced tomatoes and black olives and serve.

Serves 4

Saffron Rice Salad with Seafood

225 g/8 oz cooked saffron rice (previous
  recipe, Step 1)
2 (50-g/2-oz) sole fillets
350 g/12 oz cod fillets, skinned
175 g/6 oz cooked scampi, peeled
150 ml/¼ pint hot Quick Fish Stock
  (page 48)
½ cucumber, peeled and finely diced
100 g/4 oz black olives, stoned and cut
  into thin rings
1 small green pepper, deseeded and
  thinly sliced
1 stick celery, thinly sliced
2 tablespoons finely chopped parsley
1 teaspoon ground turmeric

DRESSING
250 ml/8 fl oz olive oil
150 ml/¼ pint red wine vinegar
2 tablespoons dry white wine
1 medium-sized onion, finely chopped
1 tablespoon finely chopped chives
salt and freshly ground black pepper

1. To make the dressing, combine olive oil, red wine vinegar, dry white wine and finely chopped onion and chives in a thick-bottomed saucepan. Season to taste and heat through. Keep warm.

2. Pour Quick Fish Stock into a thick-bottomed frying pan and liquid fry (see note below) sole fillets for 1 to 1½ minutes on each side, or until the fish flakes easily with a fork. Remove from pan with a slotted spoon and cut into even-sized chunks. Transfer to a shallow dish. Liquid fry cod fillets in the same stock for 3 to 4 minutes on each side, or until the fish flakes easily with a fork. Remove from pan with a slotted spoon and cut into even-sized chunks. Transfer to same dish.

3. Add 4 tablespoons hot stock from frying pan to dressing. Measure off 150 ml/¼ pint of the dressing and reserve. Pour remaining dressing over fish and allow to cool.

4. Meanwhile, combine finely diced cucumber, black olive rings, thinly sliced pepper and celery and finely chopped parsley in another dish. Pour reserved dressing over and toss until all ingredients glisten. Drain.

5. Place cooked saffron rice in a salad bowl and stir in ground turmeric. Add cooked peeled scampi, fish chunks together with their dressing, and vegetables. Toss lightly until all ingredients glisten and serve.

Serves 6 to 8

Note I use the term liquid fry to designate a new, fatless cooking method for fish. Just cover the bottom of a thick-bottomed frying pan with a little well-flavoured fish stock and cook fish fillets for a few minutes on each side.

Seafood Picnic Salad

450 g/1 lb cooked turbot or halibut, flaked
225 g/8 oz new potatoes, preboiled in
  their jackets
3 tablespoons finely chopped onion
2 sticks celery, finely chopped
1 small green pepper, deseeded and
  finely chopped
150 ml/¼ pint French Dressing (page 159)
lettuce leaves

1. Peel and dice boiled potatoes.

2. Combine, fish, potatoes, onion, celery and pepper. Pour over French Dressing and toss. Serve on a bed of lettuce leaves.

Serves 6

Curried Chicken Salad

3 cooked chicken breasts, cut crossways
  into thin strips
3 canned pimientos, cut into thin strips
2 small green peppers, deseeded and cut
  into thin strips
8–10 lettuce leaves
finely chopped parsley

DRESSING
150 ml/$\frac{1}{4}$ pint olive oil
3–4 tablespoons lemon juice
1 clove garlic, finely chopped
salt and freshly ground black pepper

CURRIED MAYONNAISE
300 ml/$\frac{1}{2}$ pint mayonnaise
2 teaspoons curry paste

1.   To make Curried Mayonnaise, combine
mayonnaise and curry paste.

2.   To make the dressing, combine olive oil,
lemon juice and finely chopped garlic, and
season to taste with salt and freshly ground
black pepper.

3.   Place chicken, pimiento and green pepper
strips in three separate bowls. Pour one-third
of the dressing into each bowl and toss until all
ingredients glisten.

4.   Arrange 4 or 5 lettuce leaves at each end of
a serving dish. Lay half the pepper strips in a
neat row at one end, followed by half the
chicken strips and all the pimiento strips.
Finish with remaining chicken strips and
pepper strips. Sprinkle with finely chopped
parsley and serve, accompanied by Curried
Mayonnaise.

Serves 4

Cold Curry of Chicken and Beef

225 g/8 oz cooked chicken, diced
225 g/8 oz cold roast beef, cut into strips
2 crisp dessert apples
lemon juice
2 sticks celery, thinly sliced
1 medium-sized green pepper, deseeded
  and diced
salt and freshly ground black pepper
cayenne
curry powder
1 tablespoon chopped coriander leaves or
  flat-leafed parsley

COLD CURRY SAUCE
6 tablespoons mayonnaise
6 tablespoons double cream
1 tablespoon curry paste
25 g/1 oz raisins, blanched
juice of $\frac{1}{2}$ lemon
1 tablespoon mango chutney
1 tablespoon finely chopped onion

1.   To make Cold Curry Sauce, combine
mayonnaise, double cream, curry paste,
blanched raisins, lemon juice, mango chutney
and finely chopped onion.

2.   Peel, core and dice apples. Sprinkle with
lemon juice to preserve colour.

3.   Combine diced chicken, beef strips, thinly
sliced celery, and diced pepper and apples in a
salad bowl. Season to taste with lemon juice,
salt, freshly ground black pepper and cayenne.
Add Cold Curry Sauce and toss until all
ingredients are evenly coated. Sprinkle with a
little curry powder and cayenne, and the
chopped coriander leaves or flat-leafed parsley,
and serve.

Serves 4

Truffled Turkey Salad

1 (38-g/1⅜-oz) can black truffles, drained
  and diced, can juices reserved
450 g/1 lb cold cooked turkey, diced
1 lettuce
6 tablespoons mayonnaise
2 tablespoons lemon juice
salt and freshly ground black pepper
celery salt
4 hard-boiled eggs, finely chopped
4 sticks celery, thinly sliced

1.   Wash and prepare lettuce. Shake dry in a
salad basket or dry each leaf carefully with
absorbent kitchen paper. Shred lettuce.

2.   Thin mayonnaise with lemon juice and
reserved truffle juice, and season to taste with
salt, freshly ground black pepper and celery
salt.

3.   Add diced truffles to mayonnaise.

4.   Combine diced cooked turkey, shredded
lettuce, finely chopped eggs and thinly sliced
celery in a salad bowl. Add mayonnaise
mixture. Toss until all ingredients are evenly
coated and serve.

Serves 4

Turkey Apple Walnut Salad

450 g/1 lb cooked turkey, cut into 1-cm/
  ½-in cubes
2 red-skinned dessert apples, cored and
  sliced
12 walnut halves
1 lettuce
4 sticks celery, sliced
6–8 tablespoons olive oil
2 tablespoons red wine vinegar
1 small onion, finely chopped
salt and freshly ground black pepper

1.   Wash and prepare lettuce. Shake dry in a
salad basket or dry each leaf carefully with
absorbent kitchen paper.

2.   Combine turkey cubes and sliced apple and
celery in a porcelain or earthenware (not metal)
bowl.

3.   Combine olive oil and red wine vinegar
(three to four parts olive oil to one part red
wine vinegar). Add finely chopped onion and
season to taste with salt and freshly ground
black pepper.

4.   Pour half the dressing over turkey mixture. Allow to marinate for 15 minutes. Drain.

5.   Toss turkey mixture in remaining dressing. Line a glass salad bowl with lettuce leaves.
Pile turkey mixture into centre of bowl, scatter
over walnut halves and serve.

Serves 4 to 6

Chicken, Orange and Avocado Salad

350 g/12 oz cooked chicken, diced
4 small oranges
1 ripe avocado pear
4 shallots, finely chopped
2 sticks celery, sliced
lemon juice
lettuce leaves
8–10 black olives, stoned

DRESSING
generous 150 ml/$\frac{1}{4}$ pint olive oil
3 tablespoons red wine vinegar
pinch of dried rosemary
1 tablespoon chopped parsley
salt and freshly ground black pepper

1. To make the dressing, combine olive oil, red wine vinegar, dried rosemary and chopped parsley, and season to taste with salt and freshly ground black pepper.

2. Combine diced chicken, finely chopped shallot and sliced celery in a porcelain or earthenware (not metal) bowl. Pour over dressing and allow to marinate for 20 minutes.

3. Meanwhile, peel oranges and cut away all white pith. Slip knife blade between each segment and membrane and cut segment out. Remove any pips.

4. Cut avocado pear in half, remove stone and peel avocado. Sprinkle flesh with lemon juice to preserve colour, then slice into crescents 3 mm/$\frac{1}{8}$ in thick.

5. Add orange segments to salad and toss.

6. Line a salad bowl with lettuce leaves. Arrange salad in bowl, garnish with black olives and avocado crescents and serve.

Serves 4

Christmas Salad

1–2 lettuces
2 oranges
2 thin slices pineapple, hard central core removed, cut into tiny wedges

FRENCH DRESSING
6–8 tablespoons olive oil
2 tablespoons red wine vinegar
salt and freshly ground black pepper

1. Wash and prepare lettuce. Shake dry in a salad basket or dry each leaf carefully with absorbent kitchen paper.

2. Peel oranges and cut away all white pith. Slip knife blade between each segment and membrane and cut segment out. Remove any pips.

3. To make the French Dressing, combine olive oil and red wine vinegar (three to four parts olive oil to one part red wine vinegar) and season to taste with salt and freshly ground black pepper.

4. Combine lettuce leaves, orange segments and pineapple wedges in a salad bowl. Pour over French Dressing, toss until all ingredients glisten and serve.

Serves 4 to 6

Ham and Apple Salad with Roquefort Cheese Balls

350 g/12 oz cooked ham, cut into cubes
3 red-skinned dessert apples
lemon juice
6 tablespoons mayonnaise
3 tablespoons double cream
1 small green pepper, deseeded and
  thinly sliced
salt and freshly ground black pepper
lettuce leaves
3 tablespoons chopped walnuts
chopped chives

ROQUEFORT CHEESE BALLS
65 g/2½ oz softened butter
50 g/2 oz Roquefort cheese, crumbled
freshly ground black pepper
paprika
cayenne
1–2 slices dark pumpernickel bread,
  crumbled

1. To make Roquefort Cheese Balls, cream together softened butter and crumbled Roquefort cheese, and season to taste with freshly ground black pepper, paprika, and just a hint of cayenne. Form into 12 small balls and roll in crumbled bread, patting coating on firmly.

2. Core and slice apples and sprinkle with lemon juice to preserve colour. Reserve 12 apple slices for garnish.

3. Combine mayonnaise and double cream. Add ham cubes, thinly sliced green pepper and remaining apple slices. Season to taste with salt and freshly ground black pepper, and toss until evenly coated.

4. Arrange salad on a bed of lettuce leaves in a large bowl or on four individual serving plates. Before serving, garnish the bowl or each plate with the Roquefort Cheese Balls, reserved apple slices, chopped walnuts and a few chopped chives.

Serves 4

Tuna Waldorf Salad

2 (198-g/7-oz) cans tuna fish, drained and
  broken into bite-sized pieces
4 sticks celery, sliced
6 tablespoons walnut pieces
mayonnaise
lemon juice
salt and freshly ground black pepper
cayenne
3 tart dessert apples
lettuce leaves

1. Combine tuna fish pieces, sliced celery, walnut pieces and enough mayonnaise to hold ingredients together. Season to taste with lemon juice, salt, freshly ground black pepper and cayenne.

2. Core and dice apples and sprinkle with lemon juice to preserve colour.

3. Combine tuna fish mixture with diced apples and serve in lettuce leaves which you have formed into cups.

Serves 6

Ham and Apple Salad with Roquefort Cheese Balls

CHAPTER TWELVE

PASTA AND RICE

Farfalle con Salsa Freddo

(Bowknots with Summer Sauce)

450 g/1 lb bowknots (farfalle)
6 medium-sized tomatoes or 1 (397-g/
  14-oz) can peeled Italian tomatoes
150 ml/¼ pint olive oil
12–18 basil leaves, coarsely chopped
1–2 teaspoons lemon juice
pinch of dried oregano
salt and freshly ground black pepper
freshly grated Parmesan cheese
12 anchovy fillets
12 black olives

1.   If using fresh tomatoes, peel, deseed and coarsely chop or cut into strips, being careful not to lose juices. If using canned tomatoes, drain, press out seeds and cut flesh into strips.

2.   Combine tomatoes, olive oil, coarsely chopped basil leaves and lemon juice. Season with dried oregano, and freshly ground black pepper to taste, and toss. Stir in a few tablespoons freshly grated Parmesan cheese.

3.   Cook bowknots in 3.5 to 4.5 litres/6 to 8 pints boiling salted water for 12 minutes, or until tender but still *al dente*. Drain and transfer to a heated serving dish. Add cold sauce, garnish with anchovy fillets and black olives, and serve with freshly grated Parmesan cheese.

Serves 4

Basic Boiled Noodles

450 g/1 lb ribbon noodles (fettuccine)
salt
100 g/4 oz butter
freshly ground black pepper

1.   Cook noodles in 3.5 to 4.5 litres/6 to 8 pints boiling salted water for 10 to 15 minutes, or until tender but still *al dente*. Drain.

2.   Return noodles to pan. Add butter, season to taste with salt and freshly ground black pepper, and toss until all strands are evenly coated. Transfer to a heated serving dish and serve immediately.

Serves 4

VARIATIONS

A   Cook as in basic recipe (above), adding 100 g/4 oz breadcrumbs which you have sautéed in butter and 2 teaspoons caraway seeds.

B   Cook as in basic recipe (above), substituting 6 tablespoons double cream, 3 egg yolks and 6 tablespoons freshly grated Parmesan cheese for the butter.

C   Cook as in basic recipe (above), adding 350 g/12 oz cooked peas and 6 tablespoons finely chopped parsley with the butter.

Farfalle con Salsa Freddo

Green and White Noodles with Ham and Mushroom Sauce

225 g/8 oz green ribbon noodles
225 g/8 oz white ribbon noodles
salt
2 tablespoons olive oil
butter
freshly grated Parmesan cheese

HAM AND MUSHROOM SAUCE
175 g/6 oz cooked ham, in one piece, cut
  into 5-mm/¼-in dice
225 g/8 oz button mushrooms, cut into
  5-mm/¼-in dice
butter
1 small onion, finely chopped
1½ tablespoons flour
150 ml/¼ pint double cream
1 tablespoon cognac
salt and freshly ground black pepper
cayenne

1.   Cook green and white noodles in about 3.5 to 4.5/6 to 8 pints boiling salted water for 10 to 15 minutes, or until tender but still *al dente*.

2.   Meanwhile, make Ham and Mushroom Sauce. Melt 25 g/1 oz butter in a thick-bottomed frying pan and sauté diced ham. As ham begins to colour, add diced mushrooms and continue to cook until mushrooms are soft but not coloured. Remove both from pan with a slotted spoon. Melt another 15 g/½ oz butter in the same pan and sauté finely chopped onion until soft but not coloured. Remove from pan with a slotted spoon and add to ham mixture.

3.   Melt a further 15 g/½ oz butter in a thick-bottomed saucepan, add flour and cook for 2 to 3 minutes, stirring constantly, until flour is cooked through. Add double cream and cook, stirring constantly, until sauce begins to thicken; do not allow sauce to come to the boil. (Should sauce separate during cooking, remove pan from heat, stir in 1 to 2 tablespoons cold milk and the emulsion will form again.) Remove pan from heat, add ham mixture and cognac, and season to taste with salt, freshly ground black pepper and cayenne.

4.   Drain noodles, return to pan and toss in olive oil until all strands are evenly coated. Add sauce and heat through. Transfer to a heated serving dish and serve immediately, with generous amounts of butter and freshly grated Parmesan cheese.

Serves 4

Fettuccine al Burro e Formaggio

(Ribbon noodles with butter and cheese sauce)

450 g/1 lb ribbon noodles (fettuccine)
salt
freshly ground black pepper
freshly grated Parmesan cheese

SAUCE
100 g/4 oz softened butter
6 tablespoons double cream
100 g/4 oz freshly grated Parmesan cheese

1.   Cook noodles in 3.5 to 4.5 litres/6 to 8 pints boiling salted water for 10 to 15 minutes, or until tender but still *al dente*.

2.   Meanwhile, make the sauce. Place softened butter in a heated serving bowl and beat with a

wooden spoon until light and creamy. Gradually beat in double cream, followed by freshly grated Parmesan cheese.

3.   Drain noodles and add to bowl. Season to taste with freshly ground black pepper and toss until all strands are evenly coated. Sprinkle with more freshly grated Parmesan cheese and serve immediately.

Serves 4

VARIATIONS

A   Cook as in basic recipe (opposite page), adding 6 chopped chicken livers, which you have sautéed in butter, to serving bowl with noodles.

B   Cook as in basic recipe (opposite page), adding 100 g/4 oz each of cooked peas and Parma ham strips, and 50 g/2 oz sliced button mushrooms which you have sautéed in butter, to serving bowl with noodles.

C   Cook as in basic recipe (opposite page), adding 100 g/4 oz smoked salmon strips and 6 tablespoons chopped chives to drained noodles, and tossing just in 8 tablespoons double cream.

Basic Boiled Spaghetti

450 g/1 lb spaghetti
salt and freshly ground black pepper
100 g/4 oz butter
2 tablespoons olive oil

1.   Cook spaghetti in 3.5 to 4.5 litres/6 to 8 pints boiling salted water for 12 to 15 minutes, or until tender but still *al dente*. Drain.

2.   Return spaghetti to pan. Add butter and olive oil, season to taste with salt and freshly ground black pepper, and toss until all strands are evenly coated. Transfer to a heated serving dish and serve immediately.

Serves 4

VARIATIONS

A   Cook as in basic recipe (above), adding 175 g/6 oz each of diced salami and mortadella.

B   Cook as in basic recipe (above), adding contents of 1 (425-g/15-oz) can peeled Italian tomatoes, deseeded and chopped, and 4 tablespoons chopped basil.

C   Cook as in basic recipe (above), adding flaked contents of 2 (198-g/7-oz) cans tuna fish.

D   Cook as in basic recipe (above) and serve with a truffle sauce, made as follows: sauté 2 or 3 thinly sliced canned truffles and 1 finely chopped small garlic clove in 50 g/2 oz butter, to give truffles flavour. Add 2 tablespoons each of truffle juice (from can), Madeira and port, and heat through.

La Macaronade

75 g/3 oz goose or bacon fat
175 g/6 oz cooked ham, in one piece,
  diced
175 g/6 oz cooked chicken, cut into
  8-mm/$\frac{1}{3}$-in dice
175 g/6 oz button mushrooms, quartered
350 g/12 oz cooked ribbon noodles
butter (optional)
olive oil (optional)
2 tablespoons Madeira
salt and freshly ground black pepper
4 tablespoons freshly grated Parmesan
  cheese

OPTIONAL EXTRAS FOR SPECIAL OCCASIONS
1–2 canned black truffles, cut into thin
  slivers
50 g/2 oz pâté de foie gras, diced

1. Melt goose or bacon fat in a thick-
bottomed frying pan and sauté diced ham and
chicken, and mushroom quarters until mushrooms are tender and golden brown. Remove
from pan with a slotted spoon. Keep warm.

2. Add cooked ribbon noodles to pan and
toss until heated through, adding a little butter
or olive oil if necessary.

3. Return ham, chicken and mushrooms to
pan. Pour in Madeira, season to taste with salt
and freshly ground black pepper, and toss until
all strands are evenly coated. At this time, add
one of the optional extras for special occasions
if desired. Transfer to a heated serving dish,
sprinkle with freshly grated Parmesan cheese
and serve immediately.

Serves 4

Green Pasta Salad

225 g/8 oz medium-sized pasta shells
salt and freshly ground black pepper
1 (227-g/8-oz) packet frozen broccoli
  florets, defrosted
100 g/4 oz frozen peas
4 courgettes
50 g/2 oz butter
4 tablespoons chicken stock
150 ml/$\frac{1}{4}$ pint French Dressing (page 159)
1–2 cloves garlic, finely chopped

1. Cook pasta shells in 1.75 to 2.25 litres/3 to
4 pints boiling salted water for 15 to 20
minutes, or until tender but still *al dente*. Drain
and rinse under cold running water. Drain
again. Allow to cool.

2. While pasta shells are cooking, prepare
vegetables. Trim broccoli stalks and cook in
boiling salted water for 3 minutes. Add peas
and cook for a further 3 minutes. Drain.

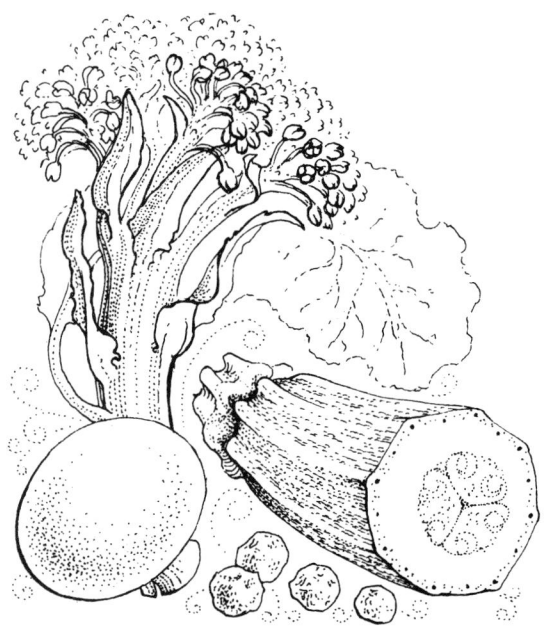

3. Cut each courgette lengthways into eight pieces, then cut each piece into 2.5-cm/1-in lengths. Blanch in boiling salted water and drain.

4. Melt butter with chicken stock in a thick-bottomed saucepan and season to taste with freshly ground black pepper. Add courgette pieces and simmer for 5 minutes, or until liquid has almost disappeared and courgettes are tender but still crisp.

5. Add broccoli and peas to pan and toss over a high heat to combine flavours. Allow to cool.

6. Place pasta shells in a salad bowl. Add French Dressing and finely chopped garlic and toss until each shell glistens. Add vegetables, toss again thoroughly, and serve.

Serves 6

Basic Boiled Rice

350 g/12 oz long-grain rice
salt and freshly ground black pepper
4 tablespoons lemon juice
25 g/1 oz butter

1. Pour 2.25 litres/4 pints water into a thick-bottomed saucepan, add a generous amount of salt and the lemon juice and bring to the boil.

2. When water is bubbling vigorously, gradually dribble rice into pan through your fingers, so that water does not come off the boil. Stir once to dislodge any grains stuck to bottom of pan, and cook for 15 to 18 minutes, or until tender but not mushy. Drain.

3. Transfer to a heated serving dish. Add butter, season to taste with salt and freshly ground black pepper, and toss until all grains are evenly coated. Serve immediately.

Serves 4

VARIATIONS

Orange Rice

Cook rice as in basic recipe (above), adding 100 g/4 oz coarsely grated raw carrot and 1 teaspoon finely grated orange rind.

Green Rice

Cook rice as in basic recipe (above), adding 2 tablespoons cooked peas and tossing in a sage butter, made as follows: sauté 1 garlic clove and $\frac{1}{2}$ teaspoon dried sage in 100 g/4 oz butter until garlic is just golden brown; then discard garlic. Sprinkle green rice with freshly grated Parmesan cheese.

Chinese Fried Rice with Peppers and Prawns

275 g/10 oz cooked rice
1 small green pepper, deseeded and diced
1 small red pepper, deseeded and diced
100 g/4 oz cooked prawns, peeled
2 tablespoons peanut oil
1 small onion, coarsely chopped
1 tablespoon soy sauce
2 eggs, beaten

1. Heat peanut oil in a wok or thick-bottomed frying pan and sauté coarsely chopped onion and diced peppers until onion is soft but not coloured.

2. Add cooked rice and prawns to wok or pan and continue to cook, stirring constantly, until rice, shellfish and vegetables begin to turn golden brown. Flavour with soy sauce.

3. Stir in beaten eggs. Transfer to a heated serving platter and serve immediately.

Serves 4

Basic Pilaff

butter
1 medium-sized onion, finely chopped
350 g/12 oz long-grain rice
450 ml/¾ pint hot chicken stock
bay leaf
⅛ teaspoon dried thyme
salt and freshly ground black pepper

1. Preheat oven to moderate (180 C, 350 F, gas 4).

2. Melt 50 g/2 oz butter in a flameproof casserole and sauté onion until just golden brown. Add rice and continue to cook, stirring, until rice begins to take on colour.

3. Pour in hot stock, add bay leaf and season to taste with dried thyme, salt and freshly ground black pepper. Cover and bake in preheated oven for 15 to 20 minutes, or until liquid has been absorbed and rice is tender but not mushy. Serve immediately, from the casserole, with additional butter.

Serves 4 to 6

VARIATIONS

A   Cook as in basic recipe (left), adding a mixture of equal parts of ground cinnamon, cardamom and mace with other seasonings.

B   Cook as in basic recipe (left), adding 1 tablespoon curry powder to hot chicken stock. Fold 4 tablespoons flaked almonds and 6 tablespoons blanched raisins into cooked rice.

C   Cook as in basic recipe (left). Fold 150 g/5 oz pine nuts, which you have sautéed in butter, into cooked rice.

Italian Risotto with Chicken Livers

350 g/12 oz risotto rice
175 g/6 oz chicken livers, diced
butter
3 tablespoons olive oil
1 medium-sized onion, finely chopped
¼ teaspoon mashed garlic
900 ml/1½ pints hot chicken stock
⅛ teaspoon ground saffron
salt and freshly ground black pepper
cayenne
freshly grated Parmesan cheese

1. Melt 40 g/1½ oz butter with the olive oil in a thick-bottomed saucepan and sauté finely chopped onion and mashed garlic until onion is soft but not coloured.

2. Add risotto rice to pan and cook, stirring constantly, until rice begins to take on colour. Stir in 300 ml/½ pint hot chicken stock, add ground saffron and season to taste with salt and freshly ground black pepper. Continue cooking, adding more stock as needed and stirring occasionally, for 20 to 25 minutes, or until rice is tender but not mushy.

3. Meanwhile, melt 25 g/1 oz butter in a thick-bottomed frying pan and sauté diced chicken livers for 1 to 2 minutes, or until golden brown. Season to taste with salt, freshly ground black pepper and cayenne.

4. Transfer rice to a heated serving dish and fold in chicken livers. Serve immediately, with freshly grated Parmesan cheese and additional butter.

Serves 6

Quick Jambalaya

25 g/1 oz butter
2 tablespoons olive oil
1 Spanish onion, finely chopped
1 green pepper, deseeded and finely chopped
1–2 cloves garlic, finely chopped
225 g/8 oz cooked ham, in one piece, cut into 8-mm/⅓-in cubes
225 ml/8 oz cooked scampi, peeled
150 ml/¼ pint dry white wine
2 (397-g/14-oz) cans peeled Italian tomatoes, drained
½ teaspoon dried thyme
¼ teaspoon dried basil or oregano
¼ teaspoon Tabasco sauce
½ teaspoon Worcestershire sauce
salt and freshly ground black pepper
350 g/12 oz risotto rice
2 tablespoons finely chopped parsley
6 stuffed olives, sliced

1. Melt butter with olive oil in a thick-bottomed saucepan and sauté finely chopped onion, green pepper and garlic until onion is soft but not coloured.

2. Add ham cubes and peeled cooked scampi to pan and continue to cook for a further few minutes. Add dry white wine and peeled Italian tomatoes and season with dried thyme, basil or oregano, Tabasco, Worcestershire sauce, and salt and freshly ground black pepper to taste. Bring to the boil.

3. Add risotto rice to pan. Reduce heat, cover and simmer for 20 to 25 minutes, or until rice is tender but not mushy. Transfer to a heated serving dish, sprinkle with finely chopped parsley and sliced olives, and serve immediately.

Serves 6

Curried Seafood Rice Ring

12 mussels
6 shelled scallops, thinly sliced
175 g/6 oz frozen Norwegian prawns,
  defrosted
225 g/8 oz long-grain rice
salt and freshly ground black pepper
1½ tablespoons dry white wine
bouquet garni (sprig of parsley, sprig of
  thyme, bay leaf)
2–4 tablespoons olive oil
butter
¼ chicken stock cube
2 tablespoons chopped parsley

SAUCE
25 g/1 oz butter
2–3 teaspoons curry powder
½ teaspoon ground turmeric
1 tablespoon flour
300 ml/½ pint hot chicken stock
salt and freshly ground black pepper
few drops of lemon juice

1. Cook rice in 1.75 litres/3 pints boiling salted water for 15 to 18 minutes, or until tender but not mushy. Drain.

2. Meanwhile, scrub mussels clean and re-move beards; discard any that are cracked and not tightly closed. Place in a thick-bottomed saucepan with a tight-fitting lid. Add dry white wine and bouquet garni. Cover and cook over a high heat for 5 to 7 minutes, shaking pan frequently, or until all shells open. Discard any mussels that remain closed. Remove mussels from pan with a slotted spoon, shaking back any liquor left in shells. Remove mussels from shells. Reserve six shells and discard the rest. Strain cooking liquor through a fine sieve and reserve.

3. Combine rice and olive oil, season to taste with salt and freshly ground black pepper, and toss. While rice is still warm, pack into a well-buttered ring mould. Cover with foil and keep warm.

4. Lightly poach thinly sliced scallops in stock made with 6 tablespoons water, reserved liquor from cooked mussels and ¼ chicken stock cube. Add mussels and prawns and heat through. Drain. Strain stock through a fine sieve and reserve.

5. To make the sauce, melt butter in a thick-bottomed saucepan, add curry powder and ground turmeric, and cook for 1 to 2 minutes. Add flour and continue to cook for 2 to 3 minutes, stirring constantly, until flour is cooked through. Gradually add hot chicken stock and cook, stirring vigorously, until thick and smooth. Season to taste with salt and freshly ground black pepper.

6. Unmould rice ring on to a heated serving platter and arrange mussels, scallops and prawns in centre of ring.

7. Add a few drops of lemon juice and reserved fish stock to sauce. Trickle sauce over shellfish and rice. Sprinkle with chopped parsley, garnish with reserved mussel shells and serve immediately.

Serves 6

Curried Seafood Rice Ring

CHAPTER THIRTEEN

SWEETS AND PUDDINGS

Green Fruit Bowl

2 bananas
2 limes
4 kiwi fruit, peeled and thinly sliced
1 bunch seedless white grapes
½ (283-g/10-oz) can gooseberries, drained,
  6 tablespoons syrup reserved

1.   Peel and slice bananas and pour over juice of 1 lime. Allow to stand for a few minutes, to absorb flavours. Drain, reserving marinade.

2.   Slice remaining lime in half lengthways and then cut each half into the thinnest slices possible.

3.   Combine thinly sliced kiwi fruit, white grapes, banana and lime slices and gooseberries in a glass serving bowl. Pour over reserved syrup and marinade, toss lightly and serve.

Serves 4

Oranges in Red Wine

4 large oranges
175 ml/6 fl oz red burgundy
225 g/8 oz sugar
1 clove
1 stick cinnamon, broken in half
2 strips lemon peel
2 strips orange peel
slivers of orange peel

1.   Combine sugar and 150 ml/¼ pint water in a thick-bottomed saucepan and bring to the boil.

2.   Add 150 ml/¼ pint red burgundy, clove, broken cinnamon stick and strips of lemon and orange peel to pan. Bring to the boil again and continue to cook until reduced to a syrup. Add remaining red burgundy.

3.   Meanwhile, peel oranges and cut away all white pith. Slip knife blade between each segment and membrane, and cut segment out. Remove any pips.

4.   Arrange orange segments in a glass serving bowl and pour over hot syrup. Allow to cool, then chill.

5.   Decorate serving bowl with slivers of orange peel and serve.

Serves 4

Compote of Summer Fruits

675 g/1½ lb black cherries, stoned
225 g/8 oz black grapes, deseeded and
  sliced
100 g/4 oz blackcurrants, stripped from
  stalks
100 g/4 oz redcurrants, stripped from
  stalks
3 tablespoons crème de cassis
2 tablespoons cognac
juice of ½ lemon
3 tablespoons icing sugar
flaked almonds

1. Combine prepared fruits in a glass serving
bowl. Add crème de cassis, cognac, lemon juice
and icing sugar and toss lightly until all fruits
are evenly coated. Chill.

2. Scatter flaked almonds over compote and
serve.

Serves 6

Strawberries with Soured Cream

24–32 large fresh strawberries, hulled and
  chilled
300 ml/½ pint soured cream
sugar

1. Arrange 6 to 8 strawberries in a circle on
each of four individual serving plates.

2. Place a dollop of soured cream in the
centre of each plate. Sprinkle cream with sugar
and serve, with remaining soured cream and
additional sugar handed separately.

Serves 4

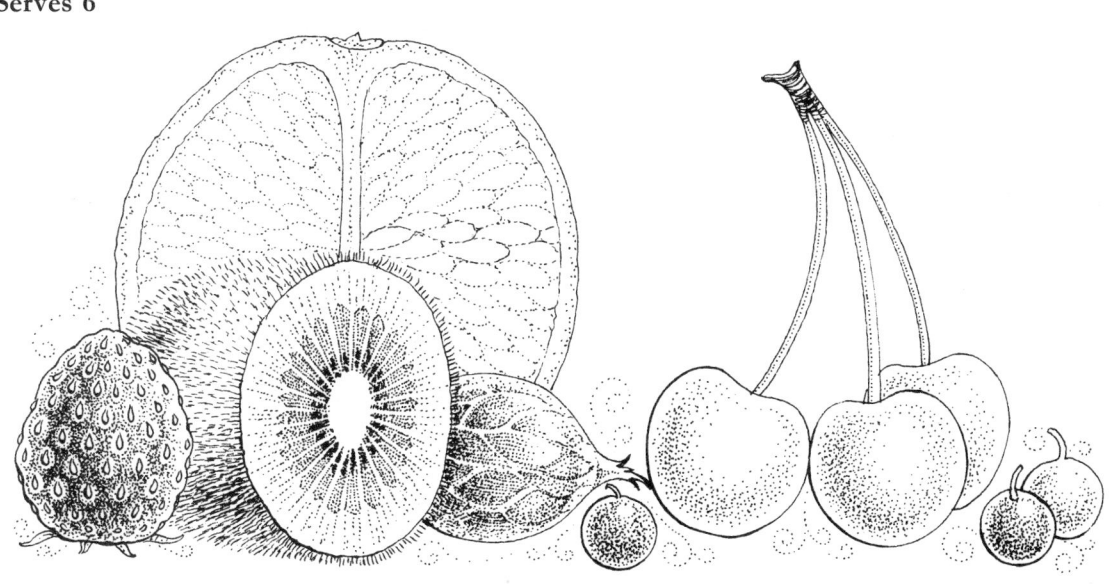

Strawberries in a Blanket

450 g/1 lb strawberries, hulled
4 tablespoons kirsch
450 ml/¾ pint double cream, whipped
4–6 tablespoons brown sugar

1. Combine strawberries and kirsch in a glass serving bowl.

2. Spread whipped cream thickly over strawberries. Chill.

3. Sprinkle cream with brown sugar and serve.

Serves 4

Watermelon with Strawberry Cream

1–2 slices watermelon, 2.5 cm/1 in thick, chilled
450 g/1 lb strawberries, hulled and chilled
300 ml/½ pint double cream, chilled
1 tablespoon kirsch
sugar

1. Peel chilled watermelon and cut flesh into 2.5-cm/1-in cubes. Arrange in four individual coupes.

2. To make Strawberry Cream, whip chilled double cream. Reserve 4 to 8 strawberries for decoration, and place the rest in the bowl of an electric blender or food processor. Blend until smooth. Add to whipped cream and flavour with kirsch, and sugar to taste.

3. Spoon the Strawberry Cream over the watermelon cubes, decorate with reserved strawberries and serve.

Serves 4

A combination of strawberries and watermelon provides a refreshing summer dessert

Easy Fruit Dessert

(a compote of preserved fruits)

Newly arrived on our supermarket shelves is a selection of jars of fruits preserved in a light syrup or an alcohol-flavoured syrup—brandy, rum, and crème de menthe flavours, to mention just a few. Keep the jars of preserved fruits in the refrigerator and serve combinations of your choice—with either ice cream, sorbet or chilled whipped cream. Add a tablespoon or two of the alcohol of your choice, to add extra interest.

12 black cherries in syrup
6 apple slices in syrup
4 plums in syrup
3 apricots in syrup
2 figs in syrup
fruit-flavoured alcohol (optional)
vanilla ice cream, blackcurrant sorbet or
 chilled whipped cream (optional)

1. Combine fruits in a glass serving bowl and spoon over a little black cherry and plum syrup. A fruit-flavoured alcohol—just a tablespoon or two—may be added to the syrup for extra interest, if desired.

2. Serve this fruit dessert by itself, or with vanilla ice cream, blackcurrant sorbet or chilled whipped cream, as desired.

Serves 1

Oriental Fruit Salad

1 ripe melon, chilled
75 g/3 oz canned kumquats
75 g/3 oz canned mandarin orange
 segments
4 tablespoons dry sherry, dry white wine
 or lemon juice

1. Remove top of chilled melon by tracing V-shaped incisions round the melon, and then cutting through each incision to the centre of the melon so that the top can be lifted off in one piece.

2. Using a melon baller, scoop out the flesh from the top, and two-thirds of the flesh from the base.

3. Combine melon balls with kumquats and mandarin orange segments and flavour with dry sherry, dry white wine or lemon juice. Arrange fruit in melon shell and serve.

Serves 4

Oriental Fruit Salad

Pear Melba

8 canned pear halves
1 plain sponge cake layer, split in half
4–8 tablespoons vanilla ice cream
whipped cream

RASPBERRY SAUCE
275 g/10 oz fresh or frozen raspberries,
  defrosted if frozen
1 tablespoon icing sugar
lemon juice

1. To make Raspberry Sauce, rub raspberries through a fine sieve, or purée them in an electric blender or food processor and then rub them through a fine sieve to remove seeds. Add icing sugar, and lemon juice to taste. Chill.

2. Using a (7.5-cm/3-in) round cutter or the rim of a wine glass, cut four rounds from plain sponge cake.

3. Sandwich pear halves together to re-form a pear shape, using 1 to 2 tablespoons vanilla ice cream to hold pear halves together. Place in freezer for 10 minutes.

4. Place 1 sponge round on each of four individual serving plates. Pipe a swirl of whipped cream on to each round, to hold pears upright, then place pears upright on cream. Top with Raspberry Sauce. Serve remaining sauce separately, so guests may help themselves.

Serves 4

Sponge Cake with Chilled Ginger Cream

4 slices sponge or pound cake
4 slices orange, halved
4 pieces crystallised ginger

CHILLED GINGER CREAM
1 (625-ml/22-fl oz) carton vanilla ice
  cream, softened to whipped cream
  consistency
4 pieces crystallised ginger, finely
  chopped
2–4 tablespoons ginger syrup

1. To make Chilled Ginger Cream, combine softened vanilla ice cream, finely chopped crystallised ginger and ginger syrup. Place in freezer for 10 minutes.

2. Meanwhile, place 1 slice cake on each of four individual serving plates. Decorate each plate with 2 overlapping orange half-slices and 1 piece crystallised ginger.

3. Top cake with Chilled Ginger Cream and serve, with remaining cream handed separately so guests may help themselves.

Serves 4

Note   This recipe is also good with ginger cake.

Chocolate Cake with Chilled Jamaican Rum Sauce

4 slices chocolate cake
4 slices orange, halved
4 pieces crystallised ginger
chopped praline or coarsely grated
  chocolate

CHILLED JAMAICAN RUM SAUCE
1 (625-ml/22-fl oz) carton coffee ice
  cream, softened to whipped cream
  consistency
4–6 tablespoons chopped praline
2–4 tablespoons Jamaican rum or crème
  de cacao

1. To make Chilled Jamaican Rum Sauce, combine softened coffee ice cream, chopped praline, and Jamaican rum or crème de cacao. Place in freezer for 10 minutes.

2. Meanwhile, place 1 slice chocolate cake on each of four individual serving plates. Decorate each plate with 2 overlapping orange half-slices and 1 piece crystallised ginger.

3. Top cake with Chilled Jamaican Rum Sauce, sprinkle with chopped praline or coarsely grated chocolate, and serve, with remaining sauce handed separately so guests may help themselves.

Serves 4

Orange Cups Sorbetière

4 large firm oranges
4 tablespoons diced pineapple
4 tablespoons sliced strawberries
4 tablespoons raspberries
1 tablespoon sugar
4 tablespoons kirsch or orange curaçao
4 scoops orange or pineapple sorbet

1. Cut 1 cm/½ in from tops of oranges. Cut a thin slice from bottoms so that oranges will stand upright. With a sharp pointed teaspoon or a grapefruit knife, remove flesh and pith. Dice flesh.

2. Combine diced orange and pineapple, sliced strawberries, raspberries, sugar, and kirsch or orange curaçao.

3. Spoon fruits, together with juices, into each orange cup. Top with a scoop of orange or pineapple sorbet and serve.

Serves 4

Vanilla Ice Cream with Hot Fudge Sauce

4 large or 8 small scoops vanilla ice cream
4 tablespoons coarsely chopped walnuts

HOT FUDGE SAUCE
150 g/5 oz butter
275 g/10 oz icing sugar
150 ml/¼ pint evaporated milk
5 tablespoons double cream
5 squares bitter chocolate
2 teaspoons instant coffee granules
2–3 tablespoons cognac

1. To make Hot Fudge Sauce, combine butter, icing sugar, evaporated milk, double cream, bitter chocolate squares and instant coffee granules in the top of a double saucepan. Cook over hot but not boiling water for 25 minutes, stirring occasionally. Stir in cognac.

2. Place 1 large or 2 small scoops vanilla ice cream in each of four individual chilled parfait glasses or ice cream coupes. Top each serving with 2 or 3 tablespoons Hot Fudge Sauce. (Allow any remaining sauce to cool, then refrigerate for later use.) Sprinkle each dessert with coarsely chopped walnuts and serve immediately.

Serves 4

Pineapple and Orange Ice Cream

4 slices pineapple, peeled and cored
3 large oranges
4 scoops vanilla ice cream
chilled whipped cream (optional)
chocolate vermicelli
toasted slivered almonds

1. Peel oranges and cut away all white pith. Slip knife blade between each segment and membrane, and cut segment out. Remove any pips.

2. Place 1 pineapple slice on each of four individual serving plates. Arrange orange segments in flower shapes on each plate. Place 1 scoop of vanilla ice cream in the hollow of each pineapple slice. Top with chilled whipped cream, if liked. Scatter over chocolate vermicelli and toasted slivered almonds and serve.

Serves 4

Pineapple and Orange Ice Cream

Chocolate Mint Ice Cream with Crème de Menthe

4 large or 8 small scoops chocolate mint
  ice cream
6 tablespoons crème de menthe
8–12 chocolate mints (optional)

ALMOND BISCUITS **(optional)**
2 tablespoons flour
1 tablespoon cornflour
40 g/1½ oz softened butter
⅛ teaspoon finely grated orange rind
3 tablespoons caster sugar
1 egg white, lightly beaten
1 tablespoon ground almonds
4–6 drops vanilla essence
2–3 drops almond essence
2 tablespoons flaked almonds

1.   Preheat oven to hot (220 C, 425 F, gas 7).

2.   To make Almond Biscuits, sift together flour and cornflour. Cream together butter, orange rind and caster sugar. Gradually add lightly beaten egg white, beating vigorously. Fold in sifted ingredients and ground almonds. Flavour with vanilla and almond essences. With a damp knife, spread mixture into strips measuring 5 × 1 cm/2 × ½ in, 10 cm/4 in apart, on a buttered and floured baking sheet. Make sure strips are evenly thin; if slightly thick, the centres will be spongy instead of crisp. Sprinkle with flaked almonds and bake in preheated oven for 4 to 6 minutes, or until golden brown with fine brown edges. Transfer to a folded tea-towel. Allow to cool before serving. This recipe makes 12 biscuits.

3.   Place 1 large or 2 small scoops chocolate mint ice cream in each of four individual chilled parfait glasses or ice cream coupes. Pour over crème de menthe. Decorate each glass or coupe with 3 Almond Biscuits, or with 2 or 3 chocolate mints, as desired, and serve.

Serves 4

Vanilla Ice Cream with Rum-Raisin Sauce

4 large or 8 small scoops vanilla ice
  cream

RUM-RAISIN SAUCE
75 g/3 oz seedless raisins
25 g/1 oz butter
6 tablespoons light brown sugar
4–6 tablespoons Jamaican rum, warmed

1.   To make Rum-Raisin Sauce, place raisins in a thick-bottomed saucepan, cover with cold water and bring to the boil. Lower heat and simmer for 2 minutes. Drain. Return raisins to pan, add butter and light brown sugar and heat gently until butter melts. Pour warmed Jamaican rum over raisins and ignite. Allow flames to die down. Keep warm.

2.   Place 1 large or 2 small scoops vanilla ice cream in each of four individual chilled parfait glasses or ice cream coupes. Spoon over Rum-Raisin Sauce and serve immediately.

Serves 4

Vanilla Ice Cream with Brandied Mincemeat

4 large or 8 small scoops vanilla ice
  cream
2 slices orange, halved

BRANDIED MINCEMEAT
1 (396-g/14-oz) jar mincemeat
50 g/2 oz butter
4 tablespoons cognac

1.   To make Brandied Mincemeat, combine mincemeat, butter and cognac in a thick-bottomed saucepan and cook, stirring constantly, until sauce is hot and bubbling.

2.   Place 1 large or 2 small scoops vanilla ice cream in each of four chilled parfait glasses or ice cream coupes. Top with Brandied Mincemeat, decorate each glass or coupe with 1 half-slice of orange and serve immediately.

Serves 4

Coffee Ice Cream with Coffee-Flavoured Egg Nog

4 large or 8 small scoops coffee ice cream
4–8 sprigs of mint
coarsely grated chocolate

COFFEE-FLAVOURED EGG NOG
6 egg yolks
6 tablespoons sugar
450 ml/$\frac{3}{4}$ pint single cream
1$\frac{1}{2}$ tablespoons cornflour, dissolved in 4
  tablespoons milk
2 teaspoons instant coffee granules,
  dissolved in 4 tablespoons Jamaican
  rum
4 teaspoons cognac

1.   To make Coffee-Flavoured Egg Nog, beat together egg yolks and sugar until thick and smooth. Combine with single cream and cornflour mixture in the top of a double saucepan. Cook over hot but not boiling water until thick, stirring constantly. Remove from heat and allow to cool slightly before stirring in dissolved instant coffee granules. Strain into a bowl, then place bowl in another, larger bowl containing ice cubes and water. Whisk until cold, then stir in cognac.

2.   Place 1 large or 2 small scoops coffee ice cream in each of four individual chilled parfait glasses or ice cream coupes. Decorate each scoop of ice cream with a mint sprig. Spoon over a dollop of Coffee-Flavoured Egg Nog, sprinkle with coarsely grated chocolate and serve.

Serves 4

Cinnamon Banana Toasts

2 teaspoons ground cinnamon
3 large bananas
lemon juice
100 g/4 oz softened butter
100 g/4 oz caster sugar
12 slices white bread, crusts removed

1.   Preheat grill to high.

2.   Peel bananas and cut crossways into slices 5 mm/¼ in thick. Brush with lemon juice to prevent flesh turning brown.

3.   Cream together softened butter, caster sugar and ground cinnamon.

4.   Spread both sides of bread slices with cinnamon butter and sandwich with banana slices. Cut each sandwich into two triangles. Grill under preheated grill for 1 to 2 minutes, or until golden brown and caramelised. Turn and repeat on other side. Pile toasts on to a heated serving platter and serve immediately.

Serves 4

Spanish Banana Dessert

5 large bananas
lemon juice
50 g/2 oz butter
100 ml/4 fl oz dry sherry
demerara sugar
300 ml/½ pint double cream, chilled
½ teaspoon vanilla essence
1 (100-g/4-oz) jar sour or maraschino cherries

1.   Peel 4 bananas and cut in half lengthways. Brush with lemon juice to prevent flesh turning brown. Peel remaining banana and cut into thin slices. Brush with lemon juice to prevent flesh turning brown.

2.   Melt 15 g/½ oz butter in each of four individual flameproof serving dishes large enough to take banana halves side by side, and sauté banana halves until golden brown on each side. Remove from heat, pour 2 tablespoons dry sherry into each dish and sprinkle with demerara sugar.

3.   Meanwhile, whip chilled double cream until soft peaks form. Fold in vanilla essence.

4.   Decorate each dish with swirls of vanilla-flavoured cream and sour or maraschino cherries. Sprinkle with more demerara sugar and serve immediately.

Serves 4

Spanish Banana Dessert

Bananas Flambé

8 large bananas
juice of 2 lemons
75 g/3 oz butter
juice and grated rind of 2 oranges
2 tablespoons caster sugar
4 tablespoons Jamaican rum, warmed
chilled whipped cream

1. Peel bananas, pour over lemon juice and allow to stand for a few minutes, to absorb flavours. Drain, reserving marinade.

2. Melt butter in a thick-bottomed frying pan large enough to take bananas side by side. Add orange juice, grated orange rind and caster sugar and simmer, stirring constantly, until sugar has dissolved. Add reserved marinade, to taste.

3. Add bananas to pan and sauté until golden brown on all sides, shaking pan and spooning over buttery juices from time to time. Remove from heat, pour over warmed rum and ignite. When flames have died down, transfer to a heated serving dish and serve immediately, accompanied by chilled whipped cream.

Serves 4 to 6

Banana Rum Crunch

225 g/8 oz digestive biscuits, crushed
3 tablespoons caster sugar
4 tablespoons melted butter
150 ml/$\frac{1}{4}$ pint double cream, whipped
1 banana, peeled, sliced and sprinkled
  with lemon juice
black treacle

FILLING
3 bananas
2 tablespoons caster sugar
2 tablespoons Jamaican rum
150 ml/$\frac{1}{4}$ pint double cream, whipped

1. Preheat oven to moderately hot (190 C, 375 F, gas 5).

2. Combine crushed digestive biscuits, caster sugar and melted butter.

3. Press biscuit crumb mixture firmly and evenly into a 19 × 2.5-cm/$7\frac{1}{2}$ × 1-in ovenproof glass dish. Bake in preheated oven for 15 minutes. Allow to cool.

4. Meanwhile, make the filling. Peel and chop bananas, combine with caster sugar and Jamaican rum and mash to a smooth pulp. Fold into whipped cream.

5. Pour filling into biscuit crust. Pipe whipped cream around edge of filling and top with banana slices. Decorate with a thin dribble of black treacle trickled from the point of a teaspoon and serve.

Serves 4 to 6

Peach Yogurt Dessert

2 peaches
3 (140-g/5-oz) cartons natural yogurt
1–2 tablespoons curaçao or Grand
  Marnier
4 tablespoons soft brown sugar

1. Peel and stone 1 peach and mash flesh.

2. Combine mashed peach, natural yogurt and curaçao or Grand Marnier. Chill.

3. Meanwhile, peel, stone and slice remaining peach. Chill.

4. Spoon peach yogurt mixture into a chilled glass serving dish and decorate with peach slices. Sprinkle centre of dessert with soft brown sugar and serve.

Serves 4

Apple Fruit Cups

4 large red dessert apples
lemon juice
16 large black grapes
16 canned pineapple cubes
16 canned mandarin orange segments
8 shelled walnuts
1 (85-g/3-oz) packet Philadelphia cream
  cheese
2–3 tablespoons chopped walnuts
top of the milk or single cream
4 sprigs of mint

PAPRIKA HONEY DRESSING
6–8 tablespoons olive oil
2 tablespoons red wine vinegar
honey
paprika

1. Scoop out flesh from apples with a grapefruit knife. Sprinkle insides of apples with lemon juice to preserve colour.

2. Dice apple flesh and soak in lemon juice to preserve colour. Drain.

3. Combine diced apple, black grapes, pineapple cubes, mandarin orange segments and walnuts. Pile mixture into apple cups. Chill.

4. Combine cream cheese, chopped walnuts and enough top of the milk or single cream to make cream cheese manageable. Form into eight small balls and chill.

5. Meanwhile, make Paprika Honey Dressing. Combine olive oil and red wine vinegar (three to four parts olive oil to one part red wine vinegar), and flavour to taste with honey and paprika.

6. Place 1 apple cup on each of four individual serving plates and decorate each cup with a mint sprig and 2 cream cheese balls. Serve, with Paprika Honey Dressing handed separately.

Serves 4

Apple Snow

675 g/1½ lb cooking apples
175 g/6 oz caster sugar
juice of ½ lemon
2 egg whites
chilled whipped cream
toasted slivered almonds

1. Peel and core cooking apples and cut them into thick slices.

2. Place apple slices in a thick-bottomed saucepan. Pour over 1 tablespoon water, cover and cook until soft. Pass through a fine sieve.

3. Measure off 300 ml/½ pint purée. Add sugar and lemon juice. Allow to cool, then chill.

4. Whisk egg whites until stiff. Add to purée, whisking again until stiff and fluffy. Pile into four individual, tall serving glasses. Decorate with a swirl of chilled whipped cream, scatter over toasted slivered almonds and serve.

Serves 4

Adam and Eve Pudding

2 (425-g/15-oz) cans apple sauce
juice of ½ lemon
juice and finely grated rind of ½ orange
pinch of ground cinnamon
2 tablespoons chopped walnuts
sugar

TOPPING
100 g/4 oz softened butter
100 g/4 oz caster sugar
2 eggs, beaten
100 g/4 oz flour
1 teaspoon baking powder
pinch of salt
1–2 teaspoons milk

1. Preheat oven to moderately hot (190 C, 375 F, gas 5).

2. Place apple sauce in an ovenproof baking dish. Mix in lemon and orange juice, finely grated orange rind and ground cinnamon. Scatter over chopped walnuts.

3. To make the topping, cream together softened butter and caster sugar. Gradually add beaten eggs, beating vigorously between each addition. Sift together flour, baking powder and salt. Add dry ingredients and milk alternately to creamed mixture, mixing lightly until smooth and well blended.

4. Spread topping evenly over apple sauce and bake in preheated oven for 20 to 25 minutes, or until topping is well risen, springy to the touch and golden brown. Dust with sugar and serve.

Serves 4 to 6

Adam and Eve Pudding

Brandy Apple Fritters

4–6 tablespoons brandy
3 medium-sized cooking apples
2 tablespoons sugar
100 g/4 oz flour
$\frac{1}{4}$ teaspoon salt
1 egg, beaten
1 tablespoon melted butter
150 ml/$\frac{1}{4}$ pint light ale
oil for deep frying
caster sugar
double cream

1.   Peel and core apples and cut each apple into four thick rings. Sprinkle with sugar and brandy.

2.   Sift together flour and salt. Add beaten egg, melted butter and half the light ale, and beat until smooth. Gradually beat in remaining ale.

3.   Preheat grill to high.

4.   Heat oil in a deep saucepan or deep-fryer to a temperature of 190 C, 375 F; a 2.5-cm/1-in cube of day-old bread takes 1 minute to turn crisp and golden brown at this temperature.

5.   Dip brandied apple slices in batter, draining carefully, and deep-fry in preheated oil for 3 minutes, or until crisp and golden brown. Drain on absorbent kitchen paper. Transfer to a heated heatproof serving platter, cover with a thick layer of caster sugar, and grill under preheated grill until sugar begins to caramelise. Serve immediately, accompanied by a jug of double cream.

Serves 4

Individual Apple Rum Omelettes

6 eggs
4 tablespoons sugar
25 g/1 oz butter
1 egg white, beaten
4 tablespoons Jamaican rum, warmed
2 tablespoons icing sugar

SPICY APPLE FILLING
4 dessert apples, peeled, cored and diced
25 g/1 oz butter
2 tablespoons sugar
1 teaspoon lemon juice
$\frac{1}{8}$ teaspoon ground cinnamon

1.   To make Spicy Apple Filling, combine butter, sugar, lemon juice, ground cinnamon and 2 tablespoons water in a thick-bottomed frying pan and bring to the boil. Add diced apples, reduce heat and simmer until water has evaporated and apples are tender. Keep warm.

2.   Break 3 eggs into each of two bowls, add 2 tablespoons sugar to each bowl and beat lightly.

3.   Melt 15 g/$\frac{1}{2}$ oz butter over a high heat in each of two individual omelette pans, stirring butter around so that bottom and sides of pans are entirely coated. As soon as foaming subsides and butter is on the point of changing colour, pour one bowl of lightly beaten eggs into each pan. Cook as in basic recipe (page 62) until omelette just begins to set. Then add 1 tablespoon beaten egg white to each omelette and spread with apple mixture.

4.   Remove the pans from heat. Roll each omelette on to a heated serving platter by tilting pan, starting each omelette away from

edge of pan at one side and letting it roll over itself. Pour over warmed Jamaican rum and ignite. When flames have died down, sprinkle with icing sugar and serve immediately.

Serves 2

Zabaglione

6 egg yolks
4 tablespoons caster sugar
175–200 ml/6–7 fl oz Marsala or medium-dry sherry
$\frac{1}{8}$ teaspoon ground mace or nutmeg
1–2 teaspoons cognac

1.   Combine egg yolks, caster sugar, Marsala or medium-dry sherry, and ground mace or nutmeg in the top of a double saucepan. Beat over hot but not boiling water until mixture thickens, scraping corners of pan occasionally to prevent a thick layer forming. Be careful not to let mixture become too hot or it may curdle; if mixture seems too hot, remove top part of saucepan away from bottom part for a moment.

2.   Stir cognac into zabaglione. Pour into four individual parfait glasses or ice cream coupes and serve immediately.

Serves 4

Note   A well-made zabaglione should swell to about three or four times its original volume; the secret is to beat constantly until mixture is thick and light. Zabaglione is also good served over fresh strawberries or sliced peaches or pears.

Chocolate Almond Tart

1 (23-cm/9-in) prebaked pastry shell
toasted flaked almonds
chilled whipped cream

CHOCOLATE FILLING
600 ml/1 pint milk
2 (75-g/3-oz) packets instant chocolate dessert mix
1 teaspoon instant coffee granules
2 tablespoons double cream
1–2 tablespoons Jamaican rum

1.   To make chocolate filling, pour milk into a mixing bowl. Empty packets of instant chocolate dessert mix on to the milk and whisk until smooth; the mixture will start to thicken as you whisk.

2.   Dissolve instant coffee granules in double cream, add Jamaican rum and whisk into chocolate mixture.

3.   Spoon chocolate filling into prebaked pastry shell and chill.

4.   Decorate tart with toasted flaked almonds and swirls of chilled whipped cream and serve.

Serves 6

Lemon Posset Pie

1 (23-cm/9-in) prebaked pastry shell
candied orange and lemon slices or
 sliced glacéed fruits

LEMON POSSET FILLING
finely grated rind and juice of 2 lemons
600 ml/1 pint double cream
150 ml/¼ pint dry white wine
sugar
3 egg whites

1.   To make Lemon Posset Filling, combine finely grated lemon rind and double cream and whisk until stiff. Add lemon juice and dry white wine, and sugar to taste. Whisk egg whites until stiff and fold into lemon cream mixture. Chill.

2.   Pile Lemon Posset Filling into prebaked pastry shell. Decorate with candied orange and lemon slices or sliced glacéed fruits and serve.

Serves 6

Fresh Fruit Meringue Pie

4 slices pineapple, peeled, cored and cut
 into eighths
350 g/12 oz strawberries, hulled
3 tablespoons kirsch
1 (23-cm/9-in) prebaked pastry shell

MERINGUE TOPPING
3 egg whites
¼ teaspoon salt
100 g/4 oz sugar
¼ teaspoon vanilla essence

1.   Preheat oven to moderate (180 C, 350 F, gas 4).

2.   Combine pineapple eighths and strawberries, pour over kirsch and toss carefully.

3.   To make the meringue topping, combine egg whites and salt and whisk until stiff. Add half the sugar and continue to whisk until thick. Fold in remaining sugar and vanilla essence.

4.   Arrange fruit in the bottom of prebaked pastry shell. Pile meringue mixture on to fruit and bake in preheated oven for 12 to 15 minutes, or until meringue is just golden. Serve immediately.

Serves 6

Top to bottom: Chocolate Almond Tart (page 191), Lemon Posset Pie and Fresh Fruit Meringue Pie

Basic Sweet Crêpes

75 g/3 oz flour
1–2 tablespoons sugar
½ teaspoon salt
2 eggs, beaten
150 ml/¼ pint cold milk
2 tablespoons melted butter or olive oil
2 tablespoons cognac (optional)
olive oil
butter

1. Sift together flour, sugar and salt.

2. Gradually add beaten eggs, cold milk, melted butter or olive oil, and cognac if desired, to dry ingredients. Mix lightly until smooth and well blended. Strain through a fine sieve; the batter should be as thin as single cream.

3. Heat a thick-bottomed frying pan. Rub all over with a thick wad of absorbent kitchen paper moistened with olive oil. For each crêpe, spoon 2 tablespoons batter into pan, swirling pan to allow batter to cover entire surface thinly. Rub a knob of butter, speared on the end of a knife, round the edge of pan. Cook crêpe for 1 minute on each side, or until just golden brown. Repeat until all crêpes are cooked; stack them on a heated serving plate as they are cooked and keep them warm over hot water. The pan should be oiled again for each crêpe.

Makes 12

Crêpes Suzette

1 x recipe quantity Basic Sweet Crêpes (left)
100 g/4 oz softened butter
4 tablespoons icing sugar
grated rind of 2 lemons
grated rind and juice of 1 orange
6 tablespoons Cointreau, curaçao or Grand Marnier
sugar
4 tablespoons cognac, warmed

1. Cream together softened butter and icing sugar.

2. Add grated lemon and orange rind, orange juice and 4 tablespoons Cointreau, curaçao or Grand Marnier to creamed butter.

3. Melt orange-flavoured butter in a thick-bottomed frying pan and simmer until slightly reduced. Dip each crêpe into butter, fold into quarters and push to one side of pan. Repeat with remaining crêpes.

4. Sprinkle crêpes with sugar. Pour remaining Cointreau, curaçao or Grand Marnier into pan, together with warmed cognac, and ignite. When flames have died down, transfer 2 crêpes to each of six individual heated serving plates. Spoon over pan liquids and serve immediately.

Serves 6

Crêpes Suzette

Pineapple and Strawberry Crêpes

1 (227-g/8-oz) can pineapple cubes, drained
16 ripe strawberries, sliced
8 cooked sweet crêpes (page 194)
2 tablespoons caster sugar
2 tablespoons kirsch
300 ml/½ pint double cream, whipped
1 tablespoon toasted slivered almonds

STRAWBERRY GLAZE
6 tablespoons strawberry jam
2 tablespoons kirsch

1. Fold caster sugar and kirsch into whipped cream.

2. Combine pineapple cubes, sliced strawberries and kirsch-flavoured cream. Divide between crêpes and roll them up.

3. To make Strawberry Glaze, combine strawberry jam, kirsch and 4 tablespoons water in a thick-bottomed saucepan and heat through. Pass through a fine sieve.

4. Place 2 crêpes on each of four individual serving plates. Spoon over Strawberry Glaze, sprinkle with toasted slivered almonds and serve.

Serves 4

Amaretto Stuffed Crêpes

8 cooked sweet crêpes (page 194)
2 tablespoons caster sugar
2 tablespoons amaretto
300 ml/½ pint double cream, whipped
crumbled amaretti biscuits

APRICOT SAUCE
250 ml/8 fl oz apricot jam
4 tablespoons amaretto

1. Fold caster sugar and amaretto into the whipped cream.

2. Divide amaretto-flavoured cream between crêpes and roll them up.

3. To make Apricot Sauce, combine apricot jam, amaretto and 4 tablespoons water in a thick-bottomed saucepan. Heat through and pass through a fine sieve.

4. Place 2 crêpes on each of four individual serving plates and sprinkle each crêpe generously with crumbled amaretti biscuits. Spoon Apricot Sauce around crêpes and serve.

Serves 4

Chinese Almond Cookies

$\frac{1}{2}$ teaspoon almond essence
100 g/4 oz blanched almonds, toasted and
  finely chopped
18 blanched almonds, split in half
275 g/10 oz flour
$\frac{1}{4}$ teaspoon baking powder
$\frac{1}{4}$ teaspoon salt
100 g/4 oz softened butter
175 g/6 oz sugar
175 g/6 oz soft brown sugar
1 egg, separated
2 tablespoons milk
1 tablespoon white wine vinegar

1. Preheat oven to moderately hot (190 C, 375 F, gas 5).

2. Sift together flour, baking powder and salt.

3. Cream together softened butter, sugars and almond essence.

4. Add egg yolk, milk and white wine vinegar to creamed butter. Add dry ingredients and finely chopped almonds, mixing lightly until a soft dough forms. Form into balls 2.5 cm/1 in. in diameter and flatten them slightly. Place on a buttered baking sheet, 5 cm/2 in apart.

5. Lightly whisk egg white and brush over cookies. Press 1 almond half into centre of each cookie and bake in preheated oven for 10 to 15 minutes, or until just golden brown. Transfer to a wire rack. Allow to cool before serving.

Makes 36

Peanut Drop Cookies

200 g/7 oz salted peanuts, chopped
275 g/10 oz flour
2 teaspoons baking powder
100 g/4 oz softened butter
225 g/8 oz sugar
2 eggs
$\frac{1}{2}$ teaspoon vanilla essence
4 tablespoons milk

1. Preheat oven to moderately hot (190 C, 375 F, gas 5).

2. Sift together flour and baking powder.

3. Cream together softened butter and sugar.

4. Beat eggs and vanilla essence into creamed butter. Add dry ingredients and milk alternately, mixing lightly until smooth and well blended. Add chopped salted peanuts.

5. Drop teaspoonfuls of batter, 5 cm/2 in apart, on to a buttered baking sheet. Bake in preheated oven for 10 to 15 minutes, or until just golden brown. Transfer to a wire rack. Allow to cool before serving.

Makes 48

Almond Macaroons

210 g/7½ oz blanched almonds, finely
  chopped
½ teaspoon almond essence
225 g/8 oz caster sugar
2 egg whites

1. Preheat oven to moderately hot (190 C, 375 F, gas 5).

2. Combine finely chopped almonds and caster sugar.

3. Whisk egg whites until stiff. Fold into almond mixture with almond essence.

4. Drop tablespoonfuls of almond mixture, 2.5 cm/1 in apart, on to a buttered and floured baking sheet. Bake in preheated oven for 10 to 15 minutes, or until just golden brown. Transfer to a wire rack. Allow to cool before serving.

Makes 24

Chocolate Macaroons

65 g/2½ oz plain chocolate
125 g/4½ oz ground almonds
200 g/7 oz caster sugar
2 egg whites
40 hazelnuts

1. Preheat oven to moderate (160 C, 325 F, gas 3).

2. Combine ground almonds and caster sugar.

3. Whisk egg whites until stiff. Fold into almond mixture.

4. Place plain chocolate in the top of a double saucepan and melt over hot but not boiling water. Stir into almond mixture.

5. Drop teaspoonfuls of chocolate mixture, 2.5 cm/1 in apart, on to a buttered and floured baking sheet. Press 1 hazelnut into the centre of each macaroon. Bake in preheated oven for 20 to 25 minutes. Transfer to a wire rack and allow to cool before serving. If you like, sandwich the macaroons in pairs with a filling such as chocolate buttercream, in which case only decorate half the uncooked macaroons with a hazelnut.

Makes 40

Chocolate Macaroons

Brandy Snaps

100 g/4 oz butter
100 g/4 oz caster sugar
100 ml/4 fl oz golden syrup
100 g/4 oz flour, sifted
½ teaspoon ground ginger
2–3 drops vanilla essence
chilled whipped cream

1. Preheat oven to moderately hot (190 C, 375 F, gas 5).

2. Combine butter, the caster sugar and golden syrup in the top of a double saucepan. Cook over hot but not boiling water until sugar has dissolved.

3. Remove pan from heat and gradually add sifted flour, mixing lightly until smooth and well blended. Add ground ginger and vanilla essence.

4. Drop teaspoonfuls of the mixture, 7.5 cm/3 in apart, on to a buttered baking sheet. Bake in preheated oven for 10 minutes, or until golden brown.

5. Remove snaps from baking sheet with a palette knife and, while still warm, roll round cannoli moulds or the greased handle of a wooden spoon. Allow to cool before removing from moulds or spoon handle.

6. Fill each snap with chilled whipped cream and serve.

Makes 16

Madeleines

50 g/2 oz softened butter
100 g/4 oz caster sugar
2 eggs, separated
100 g/4 oz flour, sifted
⅛ teaspoon vanilla essence
icing sugar

1. Preheat oven to moderately hot (190 C, 375 F, gas 5).

2. Cream together softened butter and caster sugar.

3. Beat egg yolks, one at a time, into creamed butter, together with a little of the flour. Mix lightly until smooth and well blended.

4. Whisk egg whites until stiff.

5. Fold stiffly beaten egg whites and remaining flour alternately into batter. Add vanilla essence.

6. Half-fill 12 madeleine moulds with the mixture and bake in preheated oven for 15 minutes, or until well risen and just golden brown. Turn out on to a wire rack. Allow to cool.

7. Dust madeleines with icing sugar before serving.

Makes 12

Brandied Figs

1 (396-g/14-oz) can figs, drained, 6
  tablespoons syrup reserved
$\frac{1}{4}$ teaspoon ground cinnamon
2 teaspoons grated orange rind
4 tablespoons brandy
150 ml/$\frac{1}{4}$ pint double cream, chilled
$\frac{1}{4}$ teaspoon vanilla essence
icing sugar

1.   Combine ground cinnamon, grated orange
rind and brandy in a thick-bottomed saucepan
and heat through.

2.   Arrange figs in a glass serving bowl. Pour
over hot marinade and reserved syrup. Allow
to cool, then chill.

3.   Meanwhile, whip chilled double cream
until soft peaks form. Fold in vanilla essence,
and icing sugar to taste.

4.   Spoon vanilla-flavoured whipped cream
over figs and serve.

Serves 4

Italian Pears and Custard

1 (410-g/14$\frac{1}{2}$-oz) can pear halves, drained
1 (425-g/15-oz) can custard
75 g/3 oz amaretti biscuits, coarsely
  chopped
2–3 tablespoons amaretto or orange juice
4 tablespoons double cream, whipped
sprigs of angelica
glacé cherries
slivered almonds

1.   Combine coarsely chopped amaretti biscuits and amaretto or orange juice.

2.   Spoon half the custard over base of a
round glass serving dish. Sprinkle with
coarsely chopped amaretti biscuits and cover
with remaining custard, spooning it over
carefully so that biscuits are completely covered.

3.   Arrange pear halves, cut side down and
with points to the centre, in a circle on top of
custard, or, if you prefer, slice pear halves and
arrange in an overlapping circle. Decorate with
a swirl of whipped cream in centre of dish.
Sprinkle with angelica sprigs, glacé cherries
and slivered almonds and serve.

Serves 4 to 6

Pears and Gorgonzola

4 large pears
lemon juice
25 g/1 oz pistachio nuts or walnuts,
  coarsely chopped
paprika
celery leaves
sprigs of mint or watercress

FILLING
50 g/2 oz softened butter
100 g/4 oz Gorgonzola cheese
1 tablespoon cognac
freshly ground black pepper
15 g/½ oz pistachio nuts or walnuts,
  coarsely chopped

1. Peel pears, halve them lengthways and
core them, leaving stems intact. Brush with
lemon juice to prevent flesh turning brown.

2. To make the filling, cream together the
softened butter, Gorgonzola cheese and
cognac, and season to taste with freshly ground
black pepper. Add coarsely chopped pistachio
nuts or walnuts.

3. Insert a star nozzle into a piping bag and
fill bag with filling. Pipe filling into cavities of
pear halves and sandwich them together.

4. Stand 1 pear upright on each of four
individual serving plates and pipe a decorative
frill over joins. Scatter coarsely chopped
pistachio nuts or walnuts over frills and dust
pears with paprika. Garnish each plate with
celery leaves and mint or watercress sprigs and
serve.

Serves 4

Pears and Gorgonzola

Budapest Petits Fours

25 g/1 oz butter
4 tablespoons caster sugar
2 teaspoons liquid glucose
1½ tablespoons apricot jam
1½ tablespoons double cream
4 tablespoons flaked almonds
30 (4-cm/1½-in) half baked pastry cases

1. Preheat oven to moderate (160 C, 325 F,
gas 3).

2. Combine butter, caster sugar, liquid glucose, apricot jam and double cream in a thick-
bottomed saucepan. Bring to the boil, stirring
constantly. Remove from heat and allow to
cool.

3. Add flaked almonds to pan. Return to heat
and cook for 2 minutes, stirring carefully, until
mixture just bubbles. Remove from heat and
allow to cool.

4. Pour almond mixture into half baked
pastry cases, being careful not to overfill them.
Bake in preheated oven for 6 to 7 minutes, or
until golden brown. Transfer to a wire rack.
Allow to cool before serving.

Makes 30

Perfect Coffee

No matter how you make coffee—drip, percolated, filter, espresso, cafetière, or infused in an earthenware jug—the golden rules for perfect coffee remain the same.

1. Use freshly roasted or vacuum-packed coffee beans.

2. Grind beans just before you are ready to use them, selecting the degree of fineness suitable for your method.

3. Never let coffee boil or it will turn cloudy and lose its flavour.

4. Always serve coffee with hot but not boiling milk.

Arabian Coffee

Either place 1 crushed coriander seed in each coffee cup before pouring in coffee, or pour coffee into cups and sprinkle with ground cardamom.

Turkish Coffee

Measure 4 small coffee cupfuls of water and pour into a traditional Turkish coffee pot. Add sugar to taste, and bring to the boil. Add 2 tablespoons freshly ground dark roast coffee beans, stir well and bring just to the boil. Remove from heat. Bring to the boil twice more, removing from heat each time. Allow coffee to settle before pouring into coffee cups: make sure that each cup gets a little froth formed on top.

INDEX